MW01017201

A Life of Flight

A Life of Flight

One Pilot's Story,
from Piper Cubs to 747s and Beyond

CAPT. ROBERT 'BOB' GARTSHORE

Agio
PUBLISHING HOUSE

151 Howe Street, Victoria BC Canada V8V 4K5
www.agiopublishing.com

A Life of Flight
ISBN 978-1-927755-49-5 (paperback)
ISBN 978-1-927755-50-1 (ebook)

Cataloguing information available from
Library and Archives Canada.
Printed on acid-free paper.
Agio Publishing House is a socially-responsible enterprise,
measuring success on a triple-bottom-line basis.

10 9 8 7 6 5 4 3 2 1a

To Joy,
my wonderful lifetime partner,
with all my love

TABLE OF CONTENTS

FOREWORD

A few years ago, my great wife Joy and I celebrated our Diamond Jubilee with family and friends. At the time, our son Brian coaxed me into jotting down some of my flying memories for, as he said, "Dad, your career has spanned flying over a period of rapid development – from fabric-covered Cubs with a little 65-hp engine to Boeing 747s with four engines developing some 240,000 pounds of thrust."

I cannot deny that I have enjoyed my chosen career through its many ups and downs, and have also been lucky enough to have survived some of its possible sudden endings! Many decades after its beginning though, while my logbooks have been a great help with this exercise, I'm afraid that some of my memories are a bit fuzzy. In addition, I have discovered that some of the aerodromes we operated from are no longer in existence and some of these I can no longer pinpoint their location. And so I ask that my errors and omissions might be forgiven.

PROLOGUE

S hortly after daybreak, the airfield slowly woke to life. As the sky lightened, the hangar doors were rolled aside and a small group of people could be seen grouped around a glistening new aircraft inside. When they seemed satisfied, it was pushed out onto the apron where it was parked, a knot of interesting observers trailing behind.

Following a thorough check, the propeller turned, the engine coughed and caught, then after a brief pause chocks were removed and the aircraft rolled away under its own power to begin taxi trials. As the sun rose higher in the sky, up and down the grass taxi strip it went. Finally it entered the runway, throttle was advanced and the aircraft began to run faster and faster, feeling ever lighter as the tail came up and air rushed across its wings. Then it slowed.

Turning about at the downwind end, it paused, brakes were released, the engine took on a more powerful note and the exciting moment all had been waiting for finally arrived. Moving more and more swiftly down the runway, the small craft finally lifted slowly and gracefully into the air, commencing a slow climbing turning into the bright blue heavens above.

It dwindled in size with distance, but shortly before it disappeared as a speck, onlookers remarked they thought they had seen another speck closing with it.

EARLY YEARS

I was born in 1931 and raised in Calgary, Alberta. Just prior to WW2, my parents purchased a lakefront cabin at Sylvan Lake, 100 miles north of Calgary, for which they paid the grand sum of $1,000. We drove there every summer in Dad's 1934 Chevrolet, frequently behind long lines of Army convoys. My brother and I spent many happy hours at the beach watching seagulls "take off," fold their paddles and glide effortlessly along the waterfront. Then, as they were landing, they seemed suddenly to "lose" their lift. Even today I marvel at the various birds as they cope with this sudden "loss of lift" when landing on land, water or in trees. I also enjoy watching geese flying in loose formation with their wingtips almost touching the water, or high in the sky in their familiar V-shape patterns as they talk to one another.

Dad bought a double-oared rowboat from Peterborough Boats that we used for the three-mile trip across the lake to shop in the town of Sylvan Lake during the week when Dad's car was unavailable. Dad also bought a 12-foot dinghy and we learned the basics of sail by trial and error. One fall, the lake froze quite solidly in calm conditions and on a breezy Remembrance Day holiday, we naïvely tried to sail our ski-mounted boat across the lake. This was a dismal failure as the only direction it would slide was downwind!

My brother and I created a pair of "speedboats" using two plywood drop tanks for each. These drop tanks were auxiliary fuel tanks used

Our speedboat made from two "drop tanks." These drop tanks were originally plywood fuel tanks clamped to the underside of wings of Lancaster bombers to extend their range and were jettisoned after use.

to increase the range of WW2 Lancaster bombers and then jettisoned. While my speedboat might have looked speedy when fitted with our 5-hp motor, it was indeed woefully slow and its stabilizing arm made it look quite ungainly.

During the war years, I became keenly interested in the aircraft flying overhead and became proficient at telling the "good ones" from the "bad." Of course the enemy aircraft weren't over our heads in Alberta, but we schoolboys did have aircraft identification cards to show us their silhouette against the sky. We used the cards in games which involved "sailing" our cards against the school wall "for keeps!" Some cards were just so valuable that we refused to play with them and they became "keepers."

Model warplanes were built by the older boys and one could buy balsa wood construction kits powered by tiny engines. These models were either "free flight" or tethered by two wires attached to their wings and flown in circles around the "pilot."

I was given a basic model aircraft and, with earnings from my *Star Weekly* paper route, bought a Fleetwind 0.060 engine for it. I was running this noisy little engine on the workbench one day when it almost took my finger off. I hadn't been paying close attention when the drip can behind the propeller started walking forward. In reaching for it, I shattered the propeller and still carry the scar to this day. I never got to fly that airplane!

My older cousin Geoffrey Rannie was killed on August 7th, 1942 in a training accident near Claresholm, Alberta when his Avro Anson collided with another. We were all terribly saddened, but my interest in airplanes was undiminished.

Then, just after the war, a Mosquito Bomber ("F for Freddy") roared over our Calgary home in a victory demonstration flight, cutting branches off the poplar trees along our yard's front fence and we were all very thrilled! It was a great shame when this aircraft took off from Calgary next morning, executed a steep turn and cut a radio antenna causing it to crash, killing all on board. Of the crew only the radio operator survived – he was in bed with a cold.

After the war, I joined the Air Cadets (#52 Calgary Squadron) and they had numerous model aircraft which hung temptingly from their hangar ceiling. However no one even mentioned aircraft during the year I was involved and we just practiced marching around the hangar floor under the supervision of an Army drill sergeant and shot .303s at the rifle range. It was indeed quite disappointing.

There was a manual gas pump in town and I enjoyed pumping gas into its glass tank, then draining it into Dad's car for him. When I turned 16, Dad handed me my driver's license. I was in charge of a powerful vehicle, but it wasn't an aircraft – I must have talked about flying a great deal.

I became a King's Scout and Troop Leader in our 34th Scout Troop and was encouraged by our great scoutmaster Charlie Crowhurst to earn my Silver Wings with every badge on flight that was available.

Dad agreed with Mom that I should "experience" flying and bought return tickets for the two of us on a TCA Lockheed Lodestar aircraft flying from Calgary to Lethbridge. (Trans-Canada Airlines became Air Canada in 1965.) The pilots let me have a look at the world from their cockpit windows in flight and I was thrilled!

In grade 12, I was struggling in both French and Mathematics until Dad obtained the services of a retired WW2 Lancaster pilot as my Math tutor. The pilot used mathematical principals related to flight to show how calculations applied to height and depth. As a result, Algebra and Trigonometry quickly became my best subjects, although I failed my final French exam. With no "summer school" at the time, my only option was to take an additional year of high school in order to matriculate.

While I was very sorry to see my school chums enter college where we had planned to take engineering together, I was able to take several other optional subjects during the make-up year. Only many years later would I come to realize that my failure in French put me on a course to meet my future wife in Edmonton.

Other than my Star Weekly route, my first *real* job was with the Calgary Public Library as its official collector of overdue books from delinquent readers. I rode all over the south side of Calgary on my three-speed bicycle to collect these. My initial salary in 1947 was *35 cents an hour.*

PRIVATE LICENCE

In September of 1948 with my library-generated "wealth" (and Dad's money), I rode my bicycle to the airport and began taking flying lessons from Cal-Air Ltd on a Piper PA-11 Cub. This was a canvas-covered, 65-horsepower, two-seat machine in which the pilot instructor occupied the rear seat. As a student, I flew from the front seat and watched while my instructor started the engine by "flipping the propeller." I very much enjoyed the feeling of "lift" on take-off and the sudden loss of it on landing. Before my second lesson, I had decided that I wanted to be a pilot. However after five lessons spread out over 5 months, I discovered that the "course" I had been taking was not recognized by the federal government.

In August 1949, for five dollars I joined the Calgary Flying Club and began their certified ground school course which included theory of flight, aircraft maintenance, rules of the air, navigation and radio use. Basic flight training (my first 10 hours) was on an Aeronca 7-AC aircraft, a canvas-covered machine with stick controls, tandem seats and a Continental 90-hp engine. It had no radio! The club charged just $7 per hour for solo flying and $9 for dual. The total cost of a licence with text book, ground school and log book was said to be "about $300."

As several aircraft had basic 65-hp engines and were not equipped with starters, batteries or generators, I was taught to "hand start" the engine, which involved checking that chocks were in place, throttle set, gas and ignition switched on. Then, seizing the front of the correct propeller blade with fingers (thumbs *with* the fingers) of both hands, hauling down on it while drawing one leg back to ensure one's body moved away from the propeller as the engine came to life. Although I started the engine several times this way for practice, I never needed to use this procedure because most of the aircraft the flying club use, unlike the Piper Cub I began on, were equipped with starters which were quite reliable.

We always took off and landed on the grass beside the runway in use, as paved runways were deemed simply "too hard on the tires!" No radio work was involved as "stop and go" (red and green) lights from the control tower, – after we "waggled" our ailerons – were deemed to be quite sufficient. The course included take-offs, effects of controls, turns, stalls, spins, steep turns, sideslips, navigation and various types of landings.

Ralph Matthews was an excellent pilot-teacher who demonstrated the aircraft's three axes of flight (*roll, pitch* and *yaw*) quite vividly, showing that applying rudder (*yaw*) near the stall speed will result in an incipient spin. The aircraft abruptly rolls toward the stalled wing, pitches nose down and a spin develops until opposite rudder (*yaw*) is again applied and the stick (joystick) is neutralized.

After nearly five hours of dual instruction, Ralph climbed out of the aircraft, showed me where to reset the trim without his weight, and sent me off solo! I waggled my ailerons, received a green light from the control tower and took off, completed one circuit around the airport and landed on the grass again in just ten minutes.

Then it was back to circuits with emphasis on cross-wind take-offs and landings, sideslips and steep turns. I discovered that entering spins when flying solo was a bit more difficult without the instructor's weight in the back seat.

Following a checkout on the club's Cessna 140, an aluminum aircraft with side-by-side seating and *real* steering wheels, I was shown cross-country navigation along the foothills, together with "precautionary" and "forced landings."

I was also introduced to the new world of radio communications and the importance of monitoring the universal emergency frequency of 121.5 mcs which I did whenever I flew "cross-country".

Following the required minimum 30 hours of flying with the club, I was certified ready by my instructor to be examined for my private pilot licence.

The flying test for my private licence in December 1949 was not at all what I had expected. It was a nice calm day and, as the DOT (Department of Transport) examiner watched closely, I inspected the Aeronca thoroughly where it was parked just outside the hangar. The examiner climbed into the seat behind me, I started the engine and taxied out to the active runway. Then, after explaining what was wanted of me, he opened the door and climbed out of the aircraft!

I was quite stunned. When asked if I had done something wrong and he wasn't going to fly with me, he replied over the noise of the engine, "Do you think I'm crazy enough to fly with an unlicensed pilot?" and slammed the door!

I reset the trim, taxied to the take-off point beside the runway, waggled my ailerons and received a green light from the control tower. I took off, climbed to 7,000 feet (3,500 feet above the airport) as I circled slowly around the airport, entered a spin, did two turns, recovered and glided back towards the runway. I must admit that I cheated ever so slightly and applied just a trickle of power on the approach, got another green light from the tower, landed on the grass beside the runway and coasted to a stop just before the inspector. He climbed silently into the aircraft and we taxied back to the hangar. The whole test took just 30 minutes and he signed my licence application. Shortly after, I received private licence number P759.

The Canadian government at the time wanted a pool of pilots who could be called upon in emergencies (such as a war), and offered $100 after one obtained a private licence and a further $100 when one joined the RCAF. I believe my father had paid $100 to start me going and I repaid him when I received my licence but can't recall what happened when I later received $100 on joining the RCAF.

My very first passenger was my mother who sat beside me in the Cessna. Shortly after her flight, my father sat in the back seat of the Aeronca. Both said they enjoyed their tour over the city of Calgary. I next showed the city to a girlfriend in the Cessna and a school chum in the Aeronca before getting checked out on a Fairchild Cornell which had formerly been a primary trainer for the Air Force. It was a low wing aircraft with tandem seating and a fixed undercarriage and was a very basic aerobatic machine, particularly above Calgary airport's 3,500 foot altitude. A few days later, I learned that a wing had broken off from one of the Cornells (CVV or CVY – not sure which one) that I had flown, killing its pilot!

I washed and waxed club aircraft to pay for more flying hours and enjoyed practicing landing in farmers' fields in the fall after they had removed their crops. I remember a few abrupt stops when a wheel caught a gopher hole after landing! To build flying hours that winter, I flew with anyone who paid the $7 hourly rental for my aircraft. One of these was a hunter who flew with me over the frozen Chestermere Lake in a Piper Cub with its large top and bottom windows open to the noisy freezing breeze while he shot coyotes for $5 a pelt.

Both my brother Ian and I were determined to become engineering test pilots after high school and technical college training but circumstances were against it. The Korean War interfered with my plans, as I'll explain below, while poor eyesight scuppered his. Ian had studied for his Masters Degree while living below the sidewalk in London, England and, with the high cost of electricity, the low ambient light had affected his eyesight.

ROYAL CANADIAN AIR FORCE

Shortly after graduating from high school in 1950, I applied to Calgary Technical College (CalTech) to pursue my chosen career of Aeronautical Engineering. When the Korean "conflict" broke out, I cancelled my application with CalTech and instead applied to the RCAF for a Short Service (5-year) Commission. In the event of conscription, I would far rather be flying overhead than fighting with the infantry on the ground!

In late September, I was sent to London, Ontario for my basic training. My choice to avoid infantry service was confirmed when, after earning my share of demerit marks, I received the "privilege" of carrying a heavy .303 rifle around the parade square for one or two hours.

One of the tests we endured purportedly demonstrated that we were not prone to air sickness. Strapped blindfolded into a very large swing, we were swung gently back and forth for about 20 minutes which, I assume, would make some people sick. During those three months of training, numerous medicals and tests were given to "prove" that we were indeed "officer material." For example, the Air Force sergeant checked our bed-making capabilities each morning with a 25-cent piece which *bounced* on our bed when we passed his rigid inspection. We used safety pins to ensure that our bed clothes were always as tight as could be.

While in London, I joined the London Flying Club and flew several of their aircraft at London's much lower altitude. One was an Aeronca

7-DC, a side-by-side, fabric-covered machine; another was a Fleet Canuck, a Canadian-built side-by-side, fabric-covered machine with stick controls; and also an Ercoupe, a nifty low-wing, side-by-side, aluminum-covered aircraft without rudder pedals. After I passed the 50-hour flying mark, I boldly asked my Cousin Cardie Smith if I could take her beautiful daughter up for a flight. However Cardie informed me with much laughter that Anne was just 11 years old! My assessment of women obviously needed more work.

I was told that, because of my aptitude for Mathematics (with thanks to my grade 12 pilot teacher) I had been chosen by the RCAF to become an air force navigator! I refused to accept this and only then did they reluctantly allow me to join their pilot training stream.

In January 1951, I was posted to the newly reopened Gimli, Manitoba training station (scene of the famous "Gimli Glider" incident in which an Air Canada 767 landed there, out of fuel, in 1983). We suffered not a little during that bitterly cold winter with bathroom windows that had yet to be installed!

I was assigned to Course #22 which by-passed their Chipmunk primary trainers and went directly on to the noisy Canadian-built North American Harvards, otherwise known as Texans, Yellow Perils, or T-6s. These were equipped with reliable 550-hp Wasp 9-cylinder radial engines, had a retractable undercarriage and, being metal-clad, were quite heavy.

Following an introductory lesson, we concentrated on "flying" their Link Trainer. This was a closed box containing the student which rotated about its axis while the student "flew it" and, by referring solely to his instruments, he determined his flying attitude, his altitude and his position. The instructor had a chart on a table before him on which a "bug" traced the trainee's "flight path."

We had many days of −30°F temperatures that winter which required that aircraft be driven by our instructors into and out of the hangars with the engine running. Half our course either failed or died, so I was very happy to have taken flying lessons prior to this. I was duty cadet one day

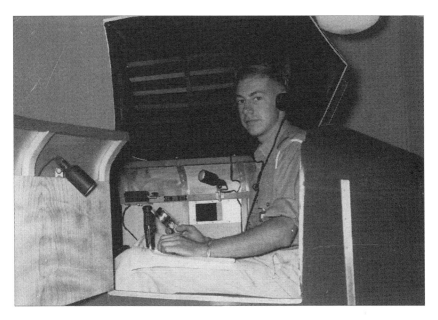

Manufactured from the 1930s to the 1950s, Link Trainers were used by both the civilian and military schools for instrument and cross-country pilot training.

when Don Z, a fellow cadet, failed to recover from a low-level manoeuvre and crashed into a heavily treed area. As duty cadet, I followed the duty officer and the military investigating team to the crash site and watched in amazement as his remains were removed from the smashed aircraft!

Then it was back to ground school again, covering in more detail the theory of flight, aircraft maintenance, rules of the air, navigation and radio use. Not only did we learn basic communication but also radio navigation. For this, we had to learn Morse code and our course obtained an average mark of 10 words per minute. It was impressed upon us that identifying stations was critically important, as homing in on the wrong station could result in rather disastrous consequences!

As I was having some difficulties with instrument flying in the Link Trainer, Dad generously offered to buy a used one and have it installed in our Calgary basement so I could practice at home whenever I visited. He really didn't know what a huge project that would have involved. I truly

Above: *My 1940 Ford convertible. Back in 1951, a boy's first car, paid for with money from his first job, was generally his first love!*

Right: *The "snow suit" was used for Gimli flying in 1951 when Arctic air covered the Prairies. Before the Harvard trainer became airborne, the cockpit was mighty cold! In addition, the suit would be essential following a forced landing.*

appreciated his offer but after some further coaching, I "got the hang of it" and became able to control both the Link Trainer and the snarling Harvard, even while occupying its back seat and totally enclosed "under the hood."

A few of our Harvards had been equipped with ADF's (Automatic Direction Finders) which pointed a needle at a radio station. After some further practice in the Link Trainer, we flew several trips in our Harvards behind our instructors using the basics of cross-country navigation and approaches while flying "blind" and I managed to pass my instrument flying test.

I bought my first car in Winnipeg for $800. It was a 1940 maroon-coloured Ford convertible which I had checked at a nearby garage. This

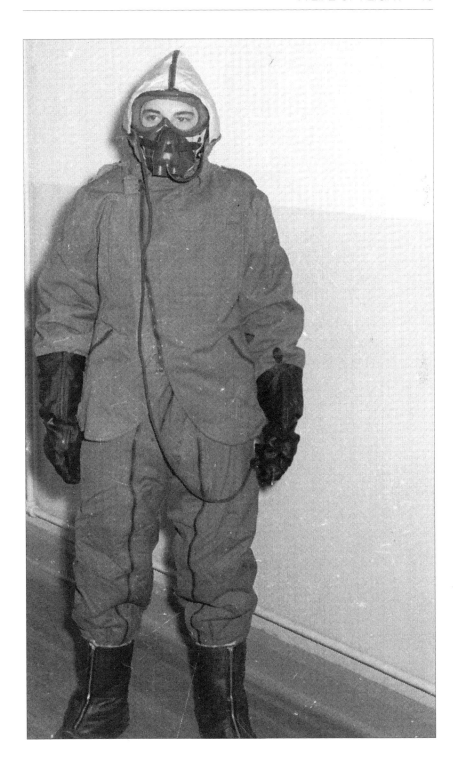

garage was owned, as it turned out, by the brother of the used car shop where I had bought the car! While it ran well, it turned out to be a real "rust bucket" and on our subsequent move back to Edmonton, the road became visible through the floor boards! But it was quite a fun car to drive!

Following our instrument flying course, we moved on to night flying and then to cross-country flying (both day and night) and basic aerobatic flying. Beyond stalls and spins, we were taught rolls (airspeed 140 knots), loops (155 knots) and rolls off the top (170 knots). Flying was cancelled whenever temperatures dropped to minus 40 and, like our instructors, we became quite proficient at taxiing our aircraft right into the hangar as its doors opened, to save our poor ground crews from having to push the heavy machines in.

Canada purchased several surplus American T-6 Texans which were ferried up to Gimli. However at least one suffered structural failure en-route while another had an engine failure and crashed, and I believe the whole lot of them were scrapped due to the discovery of wing spar corrosion.

We were kept so busy learning the RCAF aircraft and ways that we had little time for sightseeing. Flying light aircraft supplied by the Winnipeg Flying Club was therefor a treat and we were occasionally able to fly their Aeronca's as well as four-seat Stinson "Station Wagons."

Following initial training, our course was sent to MacDonald, Manitoba for bombing and gunnery school. We fired a .303 caliber machine gun from the Harvard's starboard wing at a drogue (a sleeve-shaped target) towed 500 feet behind a lumbering Dakota transport aircraft. We also practiced dive bombing, from what seemed to be a near-vertical dive, at ground targets using 11-pound practice bombs. And then finally in October 1951, I received my coveted "wings" from AVM Slemmon as Mom and Dad proudly watched, and moved up in rank from being a lowly Pilot Officer cadet to a fully commissioned Flying Officer – and so began my five-year term of service.

Given the choice between Maritime and Transport Commands (I

Flying Officer (FO) Gartshore. It is indeed a proud moment when an Air Force pilot "graduates" and receives his coveted "wings" from one of Canada's top military chiefs.

was not at all interested in flying fighters!), I chose transports and was posted to Station Edmonton with 435 (T) "Transport" Squadron which had been deployed to Burma in WW2. I arrived there in mid-October and was quartered in a private room in the officer's quarters which came complete with a *batman* who polished my shoes and made my bed! I shared a bathroom with the Roman Catholic padre and he and I got along famously.

I had driven my rusting convertible to Edmonton and, as winter was approaching and I didn't want to see snow through the floorboards, I drove it out to visit my parents in foggy Vancouver where Dad had retired with Mom. Leaving it with Dad to sell, I caught a ride on a service flight back to Edmonton where I bought a lovely almost-new green 1951 Ford coupe. After I had aircraft seat belts installed for the front seats and fixed it up with dual carburetors and exhausts and with its throaty roar, I nicknamed it "The Green Hornet."

Station Edmonton lay on the east side of Edmonton's downtown airport. To get to the control tower and the weather office on the west side, one could walk directly across the field while keeping a weather eye on the control tower for a red or green light as one approached the active runway. Our 435 Squadron was flying twin-engine Dakotas used in Burma in WW2. These were variously known as C47s, DC-3, Dakotas, Gooney Birds or C47 Skytrains and, after flying two-seat Harvards, they looked awfully big to me!

I practiced six laid-down exercises which included landings, take-offs and simulated engine failures, and learned the old rule *Dead Foot, Dead Engine.* Then on to instrument flying and approaches conducted with the aid of single and multiple radio beacons as well as the "Radio Ranges" which formed four "quadrants" (two Morse "A" and two "N") and four "beams" which were the product of overlapping A and N (.- and -.) radio signals. We also worked on GCA's (Ground Controlled Approaches) using ground-based radar, as well as completing seemingly endless airborne "compass swings" to check the accuracy of our very basic but important centre-mounted B16 standby compasses.

The military transports we were flying had simple folding bench-type seating along each side of the aircraft designed for the twenty-odd troops we normally carried during exercises. These seats could quickly be folded up as freight was being loaded, but I was rather apologetic when women and children came aboard and the canvas seats were unfolded for them, because they certainly had not been designed for comfort.

In January 1952, I was considered "safe" to fly as co-pilot and began flying regular trips to various northern airports. My first working trip was a scheduled flight (RCAF service flights 3 & 4) to Whitehorse with stops at Fort Nelson and Watson Lake and I got to appreciate our rather basic autopilot!

Leaving Whitehorse early next day, our undercarriage refused to re-tract and upon returning, we discovered that some zealous crewman had re-inserted the locking pins after my preflight inspection! Another run (RCAF service flights 1 & 2) took us via Fort Smith (the administrative capital of the NWT), Fort Churchill and Yellowknife to Cambridge Bay on Victoria Island (the world's eighth largest island).

While our maximum take-off weight was 29,000 pounds, captains were allowed to raise that to 31,000 whenever the need arose. Our Squadron's Officer Commanding could permit a further increase to 33,000 pounds in the event of an emergency! Our normal crew comple-ment of five for cross-country flying consisted of captain (pilot in com-mand), co-pilot, navigator, radio operator and an aircraft mechanic. The pilot flying that particular leg of the flight occupied the left seat and it was not unusual to be flying with a Squadron Leader, Wing Commander or even a Group Captain in the right seat. These officers – typically former WW2 pilots — were receiving a small bonus stipend each month as long as they kept up their pilot qualifications. Hence their need to log hours aloft.

I enjoyed our many trips to Whitehorse because of the magnificent scenery en route as well as its most enjoyable townsfolk. During the winter, there were the big sternwheeler riverboats laid up on the river

These shallow draft sternwheelers carried passengers and cargo from Whitehorse down the Yukon River to Dawson until 1955 when the highway was completed.

bank to explore. Their wicker furniture and log books were really most fascinating.

In February, I flew across northern Canada from Whitehorse to Goose Bay, Labrador with a very experienced pilot, landing at many different airports coming and going, and we exchanged seats which allowed me to "try out my wings!" Great experience!

In mid-March 1952 with the Korean conflict ongoing, I was detailed to fly an AIREV (Air Evacuation) flight. F/L Bill Devine and I flew to McChord Air Force Base in Washington State where we boarded two nursing sisters together with fourteen Canadian stretcher patients, several of whom were in bad shape. It was late afternoon when we left McChord, flew to Edmonton and dropped off a patient. It was quite dark when en route to Winnipeg, so we promptly noticed a red light in the cockpit signalling an open door. I was sent aft and found both sisters asleep while a soldier was trying to pry open the main entrance door from his stretcher. He was using his teeth as most of his arms and legs were missing!

It was beginning to get light when we landed at Fort William to drop off a patient and dawn was breaking when we took off. We headed off towards our next checkpoint of Grand Marais and as we reached our cruising altitude of 7,000 feet, the sun was shining mesmerizingly right in our eyes. Some two hours later, *we woke up!*

We called air traffic control and confessed our inattention. They had no radar and we advised them when we had located our position well south of the Great Lakes, and were then cleared to head northeast towards Toronto. While there was no "altitude hold" control, the Dakota had maintained its altitude pretty well by itself as far as we were aware!

After Toronto, we proceeded on to Rockcliffe Airport (Ottawa), dropped our last passenger and, as a hurricane-force storm was churning northward along the East Coast, and with no hangar available at Rockcliffe, we flew on to Dorval (west of Montreal). There was no such thing as a "duty day" for us and it had been a *very* lengthy flight! Bill's landing was not at all pretty to watch – he simply shut down the engines as we coasted to a stop on the grass in mid-field (we had left the runway) and gladly accepted a jeep ride over to the barracks.

Some time after our Medivac, I again flew with Bill on a very dark night at low level following the rail line between Calgary and Edmonton. Spying an oncoming train, Bill reached up and switched on a single landing light which so startled the train engineer that he applied emergency braking as we zoomed over him! Lots of sparks.

I fell into the routine of flying regular supply flights to Canada's Arctic stations including Whitehorse, Yellowknife, Cambridge Bay, Churchill, Coral Harbour on Southampton Island and up to Resolute Bay on Cornwallis Island. In this northern area of compass unreliability, our navigators often calculated our position with the use of LORAN (Long

Canada's transport squadrons dropped thousands of troops and their equipment during practice sessions following WW2. The Army's airbase at Currie Barracks was well used by 435 Squadron despite its close vicinity to Calgary.

Range Navigation), a radio navigation system developed in the United States during WW2. Although it used an expensive cathode ray tube, it was only accurate to within about 20 or 30 miles!

In Churchill one day, I watched with interest as a crew started a Dakota's engine which had a dead starter motor and the hand crank for this eventuality was missing. I guess we were so intrigued with this procedure that we entirely forgot to offer them *our* hand crank – and they forgot to ask! After the engine had been pre-heated, a rope was looped around one propeller, the five-man ground crew pulled the engine over a few times with ignition switches off, then jerked it rapidly with ignition on and "away it went!"

We also practiced formation flying with other Dakotas and "para-dropping" 20 troops from our main entrance door, together with their two 500-pound "para-tainer" bundles from our belly onto a target at the old Currie Barracks airfield in Calgary. The idea was to practice, practice, practice, until our formation of three aircraft could put our 60 fully-equipped troops onto the selected ground target together with their supplies *in less than a minute!*

In April, we attended the Bush Survival Training School near Smith River, northwest of Edmonton. There, we lived in the bush on Army K rations supplemented by shooting spruce grouse with the supplied "over and under" .22 Hornet/.410 shotgun. Following "graduation," we were flown to Cambridge Bay on Victoria Island for our winter survival course. After a whole day's instruction and practice in igloo building, we moved into our best igloo effort and settled down for the night.

One survivalist went to the bathroom (located in one of our earlier attempts) in the middle of the night and when he failed to return, we sent a search party to look for him. He was found in one of our igloo failures with his pants down which had trapped him when the snow collapsed! He survived because it was late April and "almost spring!"

We shot a few ptarmigan and caught Arctic char to supplement our Army K rations, although the tiny stoves we were supplied with were quite inadequate.

After much practice dropping troops in the Calgary area, I was sent to the Army's training school at Rivers, Manitoba in May and flew their trusty Dakotas loaded with Army troops in more advanced para-dropping *both day and night.*

The Army taught us the basics of parachute jumping and I learned that because of my lighter (150 pound) weight, I should use the smaller 26-foot "umbrella" rather than their standard 28-foot 'chute. Several of us had even "graduated" from the para course with their first free fall and I began training for my own "drop." I had progressed as far as the 600-foot "high tower" one day when several Army troopers were killed in the windy conditions, whereupon all aircrew parachute drops were immediately cancelled!

Britain had been training its Army pilots to return its "used" troop-carrying Hadrian gliders from France and so, following their lead, we had a great time practicing this with our Dakotas, yanking gliders, one at a time, off the ground at 85 knots. We used a line with a hook on the end to catch the glider's line stretched between two poles. Upon reaching a safe altitude near the field at Rivers or Brandon, the glider pilot released his line and we both landed for "another go!"

I enjoyed several rides in gliders as an interested observer and one day a black lab occupied the co-pilot's seat! When told to "brace," it stiffened its four legs as the Dakota roared overhead, grabbed our line and yanked us skyward.

We did several cross-country flights towing gliders which must have been interesting to off-duty pilots. We also trained in night pickups and dual glider towing, both of which could be quite exciting and needless to say, we didn't practice either of these with any frequency. We learned later that one of the Rivers Dakotas had gained 11 inches due to rivet hole elongation and could no longer fit into Montreal's Dorval hangar. We returned to Edmonton better pilots for our experiences and more aware of the Army's many problems in delivering fighting troops and supplies to the front line.

One day, from our east side of the Edmonton airport, several of us

What Mt. Assiniboine looks like to flight crews passing by!

of-duty pilots watched with passing interest at the flying show. With surface winds from the north at about 30 knots, several light aircraft taxied to the take-off point with help from their ground crew, then took off and climbed slowly to 1,000 feet above the airport where winds were obviously much stronger. They then slowly "backed up" above the airport and upon reaching the south side, slowly descended for their landing.

Because Dakotas were not pressurized, when flying from Vancouver to Calgary, we usually crossed the mountains at 11,000 feet Eastbound to avoid using oxygen. The green airway at the time took us just south of Mt. Assiniboine – *11,870 feet tall* – which is always an awesome sight in sunny weather, although we felt *very* close to it, both at night and when flying in cloud! A wonderful painting of Mt. Assiniboine hangs in our living room today and it is still an awesome sight.

Westbound from Calgary, we usually flew at 12,000 feet, above which oxygen was used. However, we sometimes practiced "oxygen flights" and on one such flight from Edmonton to Vancouver, we had just reached our cruising altitude of 20,000 feet with the Rockies in sight ahead of us when we experienced an engine problem, so had to shut it down and return to Edmonton. While there and waiting for repairs, we were not idle and completed a compass swing on another aircraft. Taking our repaired one, we climbed up to 22,000 feet, and slowly became aware that our groundspeed was just a miserable 50 knots in a very stiff headwind (the "jet stream?").

We flew troops and supplies to Ft. Chimo, PQ where we took part in the Army's very large winter exercise. As our massed formation flew over the target, it disgorged several hundred troops with their supplies into the rolling hills of a frigid northern Quebec. I also flew into many interesting airports such as Chesterfield Inlet, as well as Coral Harbour on Southampton Island in Hudson's Bay. While there, I was offered a three-foot long narwhale tusk for the princely sum of $25!

With some time off in August 1952 as we awaited our aircraft conversion course, I took my Scoutmaster in the Green Hornet down to see the San Diego Zoo. On the way home along the Coast, we dropped in on Commodore Air Services in San Francisco and rented a Republic Seabee seaplane for a tour of the Bay. We had only been up for a few minutes when we noticed an orange smoke puff from an island below, landed immediately and were warned that we had violated the airspace around Alcatraz!

In September, 435 Squadron received the first of its new Fairchild C-119 cargo aircraft, otherwise known as the "Packet" or "Flying Boxcar." I was trained on this much heavier aircraft (72,800 pounds maximum weight) with its two great big 3,500-hp Wright 3350 Turbo Compound engines. These were far more reliable than the Pratt and Whitney engines the Americans were using on their C-119s, having just two banks of nine cylinders compared with their four banks of seven and thus our rear cylinders received much better cooling than theirs. To obtain full engine power for take-off, we used a water injection system which cooled the superchargers and higher octane gasoline (115/145)

Early models of our C-119 lacked the lower dorsal tail fin (and the lateral stability) of the later models.

which was loaded in our outboard tanks, then switched to the inboard tanks where the normal (100/130) octane fuel was loaded.

One day I was very nearly killed by our Officer Commanding as he was demonstrating our speed differential over Jasper Avenue by diving beneath a low-flying Dakota coming toward us from the opposite direction. As we were recovering from our dive, it seemed to me that we were flying between the Jasper Avenue stores!

We completed many more para drops, now with 42 troops and 20 of those 500-pound bundles. The big clamshell doors at the rear of the cargo area could be opened to admit bulky freight such as jeeps which we carried on occasion. They even admitted the motorboat our CO had us fly one day to Watson Lake where he and his crowd went fishing! Later on, we heard that 435 Squadron practiced extracting heavy equipment from the rear of their aircraft as it passed by at low level.

I was quite used to taking people up for rides in light aircraft belonging to the Edmonton Flying Club and one of my passengers that fall happened to be Georgina "Jo" Tooley (which sounded so much like a boy's name that I soon changed it to "Joy"), one of two girls introduced to me by our minister. She begged me not to do anything "wild" and we enjoyed a nice quiet sightseeing tour.

One of the books I was reading was *Graphology: Handwriting for Fun and Profit*. As I did with several others, I asked Joy for a page of her handwriting. It was rather fun at the time and my written analysis of her handwriting turned out to be surprisingly accurate and I still have it.

I took Joy to the Hallowe'en party at the Officer's Mess and she came dressed as Li'l Abner's cartoon character "Wolf Girl." She turned many heads (including mine!) for she had been the life guard at Sylvan Lake and knew how to wear a tan.

She was working as head of the Proof Department at the Bank of Toronto in downtown Edmonton.

In January 1953, I was posted to the Instrument Training School at Centralia, Ontario and for two months I flew their twin-engine Beechcraft Expeditors. These were otherwise known affectionally as the C45 or "Wichita Vibrator" as they were made in Wichita, Kansas. Following graduation, I was awarded the coveted "Green Ticket" for instrument flying proficiency.

Back in Edmonton, we practiced formation flying with our C-119s while maintaining radio silence until we became quite proficient at tucking our wings just behind the wing of the aircraft ahead. In smooth air, one could draw your leader's attention by waggling your wings to set up air currents which affected his ailerons which he then felt in his control column. At night, we used the blue formation lights on top of the aircraft ahead to maintain our proper "line astern" separation.

Tight formation flying was required to get as many troops onto the ground with their equipment in as small an area as possible. From the ground, it must have been a spectacular sight as ten C-119s thundered overhead in very tight formation while ejecting 400 battle-ready and

The RCAF C-119 Flying Boxcar.

fully-equipped troops together with their 50 tons of heavy equipment into a small field.

I was standing in the back of our aircraft one day while our Commanding Officer was showing a new pilot this procedure and watched the whole operation. When the green light lit up, replacing the amber ready light, the jumpmaster urged his troops towards the two open rear doors of the aircraft yelling, "GO! GO! GO!"

Their static lines slid along the wire and as they left, the lines pulled their parachutes out. As this was occurring, the twenty 500-pound bundles were being pulled along a central rail to the front of the cargo hold and dropped out through the bomb bay doors. All was gone it seemed in just a few seconds and the aircraft simply gained altitude as its load departed.

In April 1953, I flew a C-119 with our CO to Resolute Bay, then paid an overnight visit to the farthest north US airbase at Thule, Greenland before returning to Resolute. In the sunny morning at Resolute next day, I witnessed two interesting experiments. In the first, a US naval officer stood on the frozen sea and deployed a nylon cord attached to his harness.

Over Baffin Island on a glorious sunny day in 1953, en route from Thule to Resolute Bay.

A helium-filled balloon carried the end of his cord to perhaps 700 or 800 feet and an American P2V Neptune flew toward it with a scissor-like apparatus on its nose. This snagged the cord, yanked the naval officer vertically skyward and gradually put him in trail behind the Neptune. His line was then caught with a hook by a crew member standing at the open door and he was winched in. We thought that it would be great for use not only off flat terrain, but also in heavily treed areas due to its initial vertical lift.

The second involved a light aircraft which commenced flying a tight circle at perhaps 500 feet before its passenger deployed a basket attached to a long cord which he unwound as the pilot circled. Although the bucket trailed the aircraft initially, as the cord lengthened it became more and more stationary until a person on the ground was able to either take material from it or place something into it. We thought it would be great to use this idea where there was no landing surface for small aircraft.

On June 2, 1953, after weeks of formation practise, we flew a C-119

As the air armada gathered before the actual fly-past to mark our Queen's Coronation, the loose formations of aircraft over Montreal made for some good photography.

as part of a mass fly-past in celebration of our Queen's Coronation. Approaching the Ottawa reviewing stand, a Harvard ahead of us suddenly stalled a wing and spun out from its leading formation and came spinning down through the entire formation of Harvards, Expeditors, B25 Mitchells, Dakotas, C-119s and DC-4M North Stars. Radios crackled a warning and ranks were opened as he fell through, then closed up again. He had enough sense to maintain his spin until below the hundreds of formating aircraft and then slunk away out of sight with his tail between his legs. I wondered if Her Majesty was told!

From Ottawa, we flew to Montreal, Seven Islands and Goose Bay where we completed an extensive training program which included a relief map and moving pictures prior to using the airport at Narsarsuaq, otherwise known as "Bluie West 1". This single sloping runway at the southern tip of Greenland was approached from the Simiutak radio beacon via a lengthy fjord having many "blind" fingers to lead the unwary from the main channel and could only be used when cloud and wind

One of world's few "one-way" airports, Narsarsuaq Greenland could only be used when weather and wind conditions were favourable.

conditions were satisfactory. It had been cited for being a "one-way airport," landing uphill and taking off downhill with no allowances for prevailing winds or a "missed approach".

From Labrador next day, we flew our C-119 across to Bluie West 1 in clear calm weather, enjoying an impressively close inspection of the spectacular icebergs near Simiutak as we passed, and landed there for a "quick coffee" before returning to Goose Bay. We returned to Edmonton in time to take part in the mass "Operation Mobility" exercise together with dozens of aircraft and hundreds of paratroops and their equipment over central Quebec. It was indeed another spectacular sight.

In June, with two whole days off, I drove my Green Hornet down to Sylvan Lake with a diamond ring wrapped tightly in my pocket. After asking her mom and dad's permission, I presented it to Joy who was still "dressed up" in pin curls. She accepted it!!

In August 1953, I was posted to the #4 OTU (Officer's Training Unit) in Dorval (now the Pierre Elliott Trudeau International Airport) for two weeks of captain's training on the C-119. On my return to Edmonton in September, I received my final captain's check ride and while I did not receive a raise in rank or pay, I automatically assumed responsibility for every decision thereafter made on "my flight."

During a hot day that fall, one of our C-119 captains lost his watch near Edmonton. While reaching out of his open window to catch his departing navigation chart, the watch flew from his wrist and through the propeller arc and he considered it to be lost forever. However the following spring, it was recovered by a farmer while ploughing his land, and he noticed the officer's name and rank engraved on the back. After winding, it was found to be still operational!

I enjoyed flying south to Calgary for para-dropping exercises at Currie Barracks Airport as our route took us across Sylvan Lake at 4,000 feet (1,000 feet above the lake). At the south end of the lake, we "exercised" our propellers and were gratified when, in response to our throaty roar, my future mother-in-law, known by many as "Mom Tooley," burst from her home in the village and waved a towel at us! The wife of the commanding officer at Station Penhold one day reported us for "low-flying," but my crew insisted that we had been "at least" 1,000 feet above the lake and so could *not possibly* have been low-flying! Of course, she was used to seeing the much smaller training planes then flying around Penhold.

One day, I was taking my bride-to-be down to Sylvan Lake and decided that she should take her turn at the wheel of the Green Hornet. All went well until we came to the infamous "Nisku corner" where a sharp left turn in the four-lane highway narrowed it into two lanes. In this bend, as we were accelerating to get past a very large truck, we suddenly came upon a road barrier pointing to a detour to the right! Immediately in front of the truck, we turned as instructed and entered the gravel road. Ditches on either side of the gravel road came perilously close at times as we slid back and forth! Although I glanced behind and saw the truck shatter the barricade, I was unable to talk for several minutes and Joy maintains that

I became quite pale! Upon arriving at Sylvan Lake, we visited the town clerk and requested a driving licence for Joy.

"Can she drive?" we were asked.

My affirmative answer got her the licence.

One evening, after picking up my Green Hornet from a garage near the base where it was in for an oil change, I took Joy to a Drive-In movie. Later, as I was dropping her off, I heard an unusual grinding noise and on checking the oil quantity, found to my horror that it was foaming! I took my car back to the garage next day where it was determined that the mechanic had emptied the transmission and filled the crankcase! Shortly thereafter, I went car shopping.

There was a 1952 green and yellow two-door Ford Meteor demonstrator in the showroom, but before finalizing the deal, I phoned Joy.

"Is it a baby-shit yellow?" I was asked.

Upon the salesman's assurance that no, it was indeed "canary yellow," the deal went through – and seat belts were included.

I happened to be the Squadron's "duty officer" that fall when, during a pilot training exercise, one of our C-119's propellers went through the stops into reverse pitch. This created so much drag that the aircraft spiralled down and landed in a farmer's roughly ploughed field just after the crew had lowered its wheels. Following adjustments to the propeller and locking it out of reverse, the aircraft took off from the furrowed field the same day and returned to Station Edmonton, little the worse for its rough landing – although it "enjoyed" a wash down.

In November, I piloted one of our C-119s south to the Fairchild plant in Burbank, California for necessary modifications to its tail. While awaiting its completion, my co-pilot and I seized the opportunity to take a peek at the famous Howard Hughes flying boat nearby. We climbed through a guard fence but when shot at, we didn't hang around to see if the guards were using live ammunition!

Several times we were detailed to fly an empty aircraft northwest from Edmonton, overhead Whitehorse, then south along the west coast and back across the mountains, landing at the Army's test base at Suffield,

Following its forced landing, our C-119 sits in a farmer's roughly-ploughed field north of Edmonton while its pilots and mechanics assess the situation.

Alberta. We continued climbing on oxygen as gasoline was burned, to as high an altitude as our beast could go. (I was once able to coax one empty C-119 above 34,000 feet before it shuddered and stalled.) Every hour, a new filter was placed into a canister which was fitted outside the aircraft to catch "bugs" and the used filter was then sealed. These six-hour-long flights were ostensibly "Met" (meteorological) flights but we later learned that these trips were flown after every Russian nuclear test and the fallout from it was being carefully analyzed.

In January 1954, I was detailed to take a C-119 loaded with supplies to our Canadian troops fighting in Korea. However upon our arrival in Whitehorse for fuel, we discovered that one of our propellers had become distorted. Its electrical filler, used to de-ice its four Hamilton Standard blades, had shifted and we called Edmonton to report that we had developed a "pregnant prop." They sent another C-119 to Whitehorse with a spare propeller, which picked up our load and departed, leaving us to replace our problem propeller and return empty to Edmonton. I have yet to reach Seoul and, as I had never been to Korea on "active duty" during the Korean Conflict, I was not considered to be a "veteran" until many decades later.

Bob Husch, a fellow Gimli pilot from Course 22 was flying with 426 (T) Squadron using four-engined North Stars (DC-4Ms). Unlike those used by Trans-Canada Airlines, the Air Force North Stars were unpressurized and very noisy. In February 1954, I flew as Bob's passenger from Goose Bay to Europe and he showed me three North Atlantic airfields – Keflavik, Iceland; Prestwick, Scotland and North Luffenham in England. (Bob later became Air Vice-Marshal Husch!)

It was discovered one day that our fully-loaded C-119 was unable to maintain altitude if one engine failed. (I maintained it was some jealous fellow from 426 Squadron.) After this, we were required to wear a harness with chest rings to which a parachute could be clipped if we had to bail out, although after some of the landings I had been through, I would have taken my chances! We were never required to wear a harness and carry parachutes when flying our venerable Dakotas and I often wondered if anyone had checked what would happen if one ever lost an engine while fully loaded.

In April 1954, I was asked to ferry one of our Dakotas (#975) to France. As North Atlantic weather was quite unpredictable at that time of year, I insisted on having two 450-gallon gas tanks installed in the cabin with lines and pumps, and filled as "insurance" for the ferry flight. With a co-pilot, navigator, radio operator and mechanic, we landed at Winnipeg, Manitoba; Dorval, Quebec; Goose Bay, Labrador; Narsarsuak, Greenland; Keflavik, Iceland; Prestwick, Scotland and then carried on to Metz, France.

We enjoyed sunny weather almost the entire way across the Atlantic to Prestwick and were then in cloud and sailed through the busy London airspace in cloud at 9,500 feet. While we could maintain radio contact

Above: *Prestwick, Scotland. Following our trans-Atlantic flight, our crew holds its celebration until our successful aircraft delivery in France.*

Below: *The Prestwick Airport Hotel where our RCAF crews stayed. Notice the airport's control tower above the top of the hotel.*

over Greenland and Iceland on their military radio frequency, we had no radio contact with civilian ground control over either the UK or France as our venerable Dakota was only equipped with the very basic 10-channel RCAF radio! Our radio operator was in contact with Edmonton (or Montreal sometimes) of course, and while we hoped that Edmonton would be in contact with European air traffic control, we never found out if this was so.

Over Metz, we were unable to contact the control tower. However, after buzzing the field several times, a fellow was seen running across the field and we finally made radio contact. He told us (in English) that the RCAF Metz operation had recently been shifted to Gros Tonquin, France. We had no onward charts but after we took off and climbed up a bit, we were able to contact military radar control who directed us to the Gros Tonquin airfield thirty minutes away and landed there with our 900 gallons of fuel brought all the way from Edmonton.

Not only did we not have proper radio, we had not been advised to carry either passports or return tickets! We were however able to use our Canadian money in both France and England! We boarded a train, did some sightseeing and took a full week to return to North Luffenham, England where we caught a ride home on another noisy North Star.

On May 29th 1954, I married my beautiful Joy at the Sylvan Lake church we had both attended. The minister who had introduced us performed the ceremony and following the reception, the two of us set off on our honeymoon to Vancouver. Upon arrival, I developed a painful ear infection from swimming in a hot spring's pool and spent a week in the Shaughnessy Military Hospital. With only penicillin available, the painful infection migrated to the other ear – my "honeymoon" had to be extended yet another week and I lost ten pounds.

Our squadron received several more C-119s and our good old Dakotas were being phased out. My last flight on one occurred in August, shortly after I had passed the 2,000 flying hour mark, 850 of which were on Dakotas. Thereafter, all squadron flying with its scheduled services to the north as well as para drop exercises was carried out using C-119s.

Above: *A small but meaningful wedding service, followed by a celebration with families and friends. My bride's name was actually Georgina (Georgie for short) but I changed it to "My Joy."*

Below: *En route in our two-tone Ford Meteor to my honeymoon date with the hospital!*

Joy and I rented a basement apartment on Edmonton's east side, purchased some furniture from the previous renter and spent that lingering Fall and Christmas together. Telephone lines were unavailable and Joy was plagued with morning sickness so had to give up her banking career while I was kept very busy flying – so all was not what we had expected of our early marriage.

In early 1955, my logbook showed 850 hours flying the Dakota and 1,163 hours on the C-119 with 435 Squadron when I was notified that I had been transferred from Transport to Training Command. Despite protests, I was ordered to Centralia, Ontario to attend SIT (School of Instructional Technique), then to FIS (Flying Instructor's School) in Trenton. We had an emergency phone line installed at our apartment and my mother came to assist but I regretfully left Edmonton on February 28th, just two days before Ian, our first son was born. The military was sometimes a very hard-hearted task master.

Shortly after starting my instructor's training, I was asked to take a C-119 to Great Whale River (later known as Poste-de-la-Baleine) on the eastern shore of Hudson's Bay. (For those interested, it is now known as Kuujjuarapik.) They had constructed a rough semi-prepared gravel airstrip there and needed an experienced pilot to drop off some building materials. Our landing on this rocky strip left us all shaking for quite some time after the aircraft had stopped, and our subsequent take-off was the roughest I have ever experienced. I can't imagine what it would have been like for those sitting in the back of the aircraft! My crew and I wondered just how many more hours this aircraft would be able to hold together before it simply fell apart.

Joy was unable to stay in the apartment with our new baby, so had our furniture stored and drove down to Sylvan Lake to be with Mom Tooley. But I missed my lovely wife and was eager to see our new son, and so begged her to join me in Trenton. Trans-Canada Air Lines (TCA) had, as its name implied, a cross-country flight which left Edmonton some time after midnight and after hopping across Canada, arrived in Toronto after lunch! Thus, six weeks after I left her, Joy arrived with Ian

Two months after he was born in 1955, Ian got to meet his Daddy, in Trenton. Ian was our first child. It was indeed an exhilarating experience!

who had been "as good as gold," following the very noisy North Star flight. After a desperately short nap, both were introduced to all my many aunts and uncles who were living in Toronto.

As our two-tone Ford was at Sylvan Lake, I bought a 1940 Austin A40 (with "arms" for turn signals) and we settled into our "new home," a converted barn in Trenton, for a few months. It was all that was available at the time but it had a stove in the kitchen, a sink and washing machine in the living room together with an ant colony, and a bed and bathroom in the attic. What more could we possibly want?

Following the SIT course, our FIS course became more interesting as our instructors piled on the "mistakes" that students were liable to make. Our flying became good enough to demonstrate take-offs from the rear cockpit "blind" (on instruments "under the hood") once we were lined up on the runway. One doesn't realize just what rudder forces are required to control 550 wild horses until taking off blind as the tail comes up and torque turns the aircraft. We were also taught to perfect aerobatics, at least as much as the heavy Harvard allowed, with cuban eights, rolls off the top and eight point rolls.

We drove back to Sylvan Lake in glorious weather while firing sunflower seeds through the Austin's sun roof. Wee Ian was crammed into a bassinet on the back seat and again, was "as good as gold" but we managed to plug several toilets along the way with his "flush-a-bye" diapers which didn't quite live up to their name.

I was told that I could expect to be posted to a training school and requested a posting to either the one at Penhold or Claresholm. Instead, I was ordered to #2 FTS (Flying Training School) at CFB Moose Jaw in July. Typical military!

This was shortly after a TCA North Star had collided with a Harvard trainer. Following a short visit with my parents in Vancouver, I left our Austin with Dad to sell, picked up my family in Sylvan Lake and we settled in the rented basement of a private home in Moose Jaw.

In Moose Jaw, I was assigned to "F" Flight and found it interesting to teach brand new students the art of flying "from the ground up" on those

Harvard aircraft, just as most of my own Course #22 had been taught. From the back seat, we taught our students basic flying skills and basic aerobatics and also kept our proficiency up by flying with other instructors. This included instrument flying "under the hood" from take-off to the approach-to-land and included aerobatics both visually and also under the hood with gyros set on 000/180 for rolls and 090/270 for loops in order to "roll around" our spinning gyros.

We were allowed to fly a Harvard almost any time, as well as the twin-engine Beechcraft D-18 Expeditor on request. I much enjoyed flying a Harvard alone on a summer day when fluffy white cumulus clouds were overhead. One could play tag with those fluffy clouds, chasing around them, over them and through them and I practised basic aerobatics on instruments in the larger ones. Interesting to look up at a cloud above you when you are on your back, and indeed a wonder that none of us saw another aircraft as we cut around and through the clouds, but the sky was big and we were quite small.

All went well for the first few months until we were sent groups of NATO students and quickly found that some of them were particularly dangerous, for they could not be failed (which would send the fellow home in disgrace and cause diplomatic awkwardness). Towards the end of my Air Force career, one of them nearly killed us both as we were flying over Regina Beach when he froze during a practice spin. Frantically, I tried to get him to either relax the death grip he had on his control stick or ease off on the lock he had on one rudder pedal.

As the ground spun around and around rising to meet us, I pulled my short control stick from its socket and jabbed his head with it! He shook his head, relaxed his grip just a bit and, as I bent down to return my stick to its socket with trembling hands, the Harvard recovered itself at a very low altitude between the hills of Regina Beach! This flight very nearly ended my life as well as my career.

They weren't all bad, of course, and one day a student experienced an engine failure while flying by himself over Johnstone Lake (also called Old Wives Lake) 15 miles southwest of Moose Jaw. Receiving his

Harvards over Johnstone Lake, southwest of Moose Jaw.

"MayDay" call, the tower instructed him to put his flaps down and land "wheels up" on the lake, which he did. Once down safely on the shallow lake, he was told to lower his wheels and the Harvard just sat there in the middle of the lake with its wheels on the bottom while the authorities found a boat to lift him off. He didn't even get his feet wet!

I had never held a civilian Commercial Flying Licence, but felt the need of one and one day flew one of our Expeditors to Winnipeg and there wrote the five required exams for my ATR (Airline Transport Rating), the top commercial licence. During the exam, I pointed out to the examining officer that I wasn't able to complete one of the written questions on navigation until I was provided with a true airspeed for the projected flight which, after much haggling, he did and I passed.

In April, a fellow instructor and I flew an Expeditor to Regina where we picked up our flying examiner. On the subsequent flying test, my fellow pilot forgot to close his cowl flaps just before take-off and we suffered through an amazing low level cross-country ride on the "live" engine until this was pointed out to him. Cowl flaps are opened to admit more air to the engines while taxiing as little cooling air flows over the cylinders, but they provide a great deal of unacceptable drag when airborne. As that was unacceptable, we immediately returned to Regina, dropped the inspector and flew back to Moose Jaw. The following month, we returned to Regina and both of us passed our instrument rides, thus earning our civilian ATRs with instrument endorsements. My ATR licence is #721.

On May 31st, with our instructors flying from the front seats, we formed our Harvards into a very tight 36-plane formation and then accomplished a great fly-past by the Moose Jaw control tower in a *very* low and *very* noisy salute.

Following six years of military service, I was offered both a promotion to Flight Lieutenant and a 20-year permanent commission as an inducement to remain in the Service. However I requested and received my discharge from the RCAF. As we drove away from Moose Jaw for the last time in July of 1956, we heard on the radio that one of my students had killed himself by flying into a barn.

INSTRUCTING

L eaving my family at Sylvan Lake again with Mom Tooley, I caught a ride in an Air Force C-119 to Vancouver and, with 3,100 flying hours, applied for my civilian Instructor Rating to enable me to teach basic flying on "civvy street." After being tested by the chief instructor at the Aero Club of BC, I was granted a basic Category 3 Instructor's Rating and my logbook thereafter became filled with short 15-minute to 2-hour-long flights in Fleet Canucks, Cessna 140s and Piper Tri-Pacers, flying with students to such exotic destinations as Chilliwack, Langley, Powell River and Alberni.

In August I was sent with two aircraft to manage the club's satellite schools at Port Alberni and Westview/Powell River. After initial work with very good students (including a truly excellent one from the RCMP), I was able to go swimming in the Alberni Canal while at the same time "supervising" their circuits and landings. One day I took an excellent student flying our other aircraft in formation beside me from Alberni on over Cameron Lake. Once over the ocean, we descended together through local cloud and landed at Westview. It was indeed a pleasure to have students who were not "drafted" and were most eager to learn.

One evening, after leaving Alberni in fading twilight for Vancouver, my generator failed and shortly after that, the battery died, leaving my student and I without lights or radio. I was forced to make a night landing NORDO (no radio) at the Vancouver International Airport and, while I got chewed out by the tower operator, I still can see no option. My logbook shows *177 entries* with just 119 hours of flying in August. Instructing is certainly one way to fill up a pilot's log book.

I learned to fly a Cessna 140 on floats from Helen Harrison, an awesome trans-Atlantic transport pilot who had delivered everything from Spitfires to Lancaster bombers during the war by flying them *solo* across the Atlantic. With instructor's ratings in many countries, Helen is a member of Canada's Aviation Hall of Fame.

With my brand new Float endorsement, I flew replacement film to CBC crews who were filming the Squamish River flood that year. While docking in Squamish, I was busy dodging floating logs when an inebriated man on the dock tried to assist me, missed catching my dangling line, and ended up in the water.

With my parents in a Cessna 170 floatplane, I quite disgraced myself on my birthday by trying to take off beside Thetis Island with my water rudders still down which quite neatly prevented my take-off. Experience is indeed a great teacher.

Of course I missed my bride and new son. Joy was the Red Cross swimming examiner at Sylvan Lake that summer and after she finished, I flew to Calgary where Joy and baby Ian met me with bags packed. We drove to Vancouver where I had rented a fairly new furnished house which shortly thereafter, we discovered was haunted! I knew that they have old haunted houses in England, but didn't realize that we also have them in Canada. The owner's spouse had passed away and the ghost kept returning (through the locked front door!) to check on the silverware in the china cabinet drawer before vanishing. After we left the following year, we asked the new renters about the ghost and they informed us that it was indeed still roving about.

In the fall of 1956, I applied and was offered interviews with both TCA and CPA (Canadian Pacific Air Lines). I flew via TCA to Montreal to be interviewed and, while stripped naked in a room waiting for my medical, I discovered a picture with a hole in the wall behind it! Shortly thereafter, I received my examination.

Returning to Vancouver, following my checkup by a CPA doctor, I was offered a job flying their DC-3s. I chose CPA over TCA as: #1, Vancouver was much closer to "home" than Montreal (or Halifax); #2, I had flown DC-3s which they were using; and #3, I would also much rather fly around mountains than through Atlantic fog! As an added inducement, I was told that captain's jobs were available to experienced pilots flying their big C46 Curtis Commandos which were supplying Canada's DEW Line.

As Joy had never before been in a float plane, I took her flying one day in one of the club's Cessnas. On returning to Vancouver, we found it to be covered by low cloud. I tuned in their radio beacon and, with its identifier ringing in my ears, let down through the low cloud, broke out at 400 feet over the Fraser River and made a water landing – illegally, but quite safely.

I also flew with a friend in a float plane up Indian Arm for a fishing trip. After landing, we tied up to a private dock. As we laid out our fishing gear on the dock, our lines became tangled and we spent the entire two hours patiently untangling them! It certainly was a long time before I tried fishing again.

Those were indeed interesting times, although the income wasn't great. I also flew with Len Milne, a DOT (Department of Transport) examiner, who awarded me an upgraded Instructor's Category 2 rating.

CANADIAN PACIFIC AIRLINES

In January 1957, earning the grand sum of $260 per month "training pay," I had a four-hour familiarization flight as a first officer in one of their DC-3s and then flew one return trip to Prince George. The passenger terminal, on the south side of the main Vancouver airport runway, was a friendly place and we much enjoyed CPA's very helpful ground staff.

Following that DC-3 flight, I was offered a job flying as co-pilot in their overseas DC-6 operation. On February 21st, following a two-week instrument course in their Link Trainer, I had a two-hour familiarization ride around Vancouver. While I had flown heavy twin-engine aircraft, the DC-6 was my first experience with four. Flying with two 2,500-hp engines shut down on one side of the DC-6 seemed roughly equivalent to shutting down a single 3,500-hp engine on the C-119. In addition, the DC-6 was my first experience with pressurization which enabled flights as high as 25,000 feet without wearing those cumbersome oxygen masks.

In preparation for international flying, all CPA crews were required to be vaccinated against such diseases as typhoid, yellow fever, tetanus, small pox, diphtheria, cholera and scarlet fever. One of our loathsome shots was TABD&T (whatever that was!). Some shots were required to be done yearly and some every six months. While most were trouble free, cholera provoked such a reaction that several of our flight crew had to be hospitalized and treated for several days. Our caring CPA Doc Wilson agreed that this was non-productive and ended up by giving a very weakened dose, enabling us all to continue flying. I never heard of anyone contracting cholera while I was employed with CPA.

On February 24th I flew a familiarization flight as a wide-eyed second officer on CPA's NOPAC (North Pacific – Tokyo and Hong Kong) run which made a normal refuelling stop at Cold Bay, Alaska. Tokyo had a great CPA staff house with friendly workers and good beds. The food was very good but the sight of a man neatly clipping the small lawn with what looked like nail clippers was a real eye-opener!

Hong Kong's Kai Tak airport was a "fun" place to land, particularly when its normally gusty southerly winds were blowing. Its celebrated "checkerboard approach" was an interesting one. As we descended, we made our way past many high-rise buildings and over the large hilltop-mounted checkerboard before taking a sharp right turn, then landed while "crabbing" into the wind. While the trip (for me) took just a week, I spent 60 hours in the air, 24 hours of them at night. It might have been less but, en route to Cold Bay on our way home, we were forced to make an additional stop at Shemya in the Aleutians for more fuel.

Our crew consisted of a captain, two co-pilots, one or two navigators, three stewardesses and a mechanic who handled the refuelling chores. As the powers that be decided that pilots could now operate the high frequency (HF) radio for communication with ground operators, their radio operators and their Morse keys had recently been removed. While the HF was often quite noisy due to atmospherics, heavy radio static could always be expected anywhere near thunderstorms or during solar flares and it was all very hard on the ears.

We carried 62 passengers, with first class passengers occupying the rear of the aircraft which was quieter. Each set of four seats in first class made into a lower bunk with a pullman-style upper berth above. Flight crews could utilize these upper berths for a rest whenever passengers declined to pay for them. In addition, whenever the exclusive "club class" compartment aft of the cockpit on the port side was available, it could be used for rest by the flight crew.

Joy and I purchased a brand new six-room bungalow in Richmond

Kai Tak Airport Hong Kong – a sometimes challenging airport. One's first arrival is indeed eye-opening!

(on Lulu Island) that spring. Mom and Dad kindly gave us an automatic washer and dryer and a new TV (two channels of black and white with rabbit ears!). We paid $12,300 for the house and moved in after the RCAF paid to move our furniture from Edmonton. We had the front lawn seeded and the back yard fenced and Joy was pleasantly surprised at the rapid growth of her garden! It also seemed that for several months of the year, I had to cut the grass every few days with our hand mower. Our Gilmore Park subdivision had previously been farm acreage and was blessed with very rich delta soil.

After receiving my final check ride in March, I began operating regular runs to Tokyo as a fully-qualified Second Officer. It was a real privilege to fly with so many WW2 flying veterans, although most of them refused to elaborate on their varied wartime experiences. Many had more than 1,000 hours of Lancaster or Spitfire time over Europe and some had been shot down, experienced a ditching or suffered in prison camps.

I learned that in late August of the previous year (1956), one of our crews had missed its approach at Cold Bay. On their climbing turn to avoid the hills ahead, the pilot not flying had fully raised the flaps and without their lift, the aircraft sank and hit the ground. We heard that Bob, the first officer who was occupying the club compartment's bunk at the time, had decapitated the captain as he shot feet-first through the cockpit and ended up in the mud but had somehow survived and flew again! Decades later and after Bob's death, his wife Bea remarried and it happened that she was our next door neighbour when we moved to Victoria. Bea was a noted landscape painter and one of her wonderful paintings hangs today in our living room.

With practice in the good old wartime Link Trainer, we became quite proficient in radio communication and in radio navigation utilizing SRA's (Standard Range Approaches). In the SRA, we located our position by finding one of the radio station's four aural "beams" and tracking in on it to the station. After passing overhead its "aural null," we used one of its beams to track outbound, complete a procedure turn and track inbound while descending to the radio station followed by a timed descent to our minimum altitude where we either completed a visual landing – or overshot and proceeded to our alternate aerodrome.

We were also trained in the use of RMI's (Radio Magnetic Indicators), VOR's (Visual Omni Ranges), RAA's (Radar Assisted Approaches) and the recent ILS (Instrument Landing System) then being installed at major airports. With them, we could accomplish approaches to minimum altitudes as low as two hundred feet! I received 80 hours of Link instruction during my first year with CPA.

My second trip went via Cold Bay only as far as Tokyo where we "slipped crews," and I only completed 36 hours of uneventful flying that week. We waited four days in Tokyo while the previous slipped crew took our flight on to Hong Kong and back, and then my third trip (also 36 flying hours) routed via Anchorage and then Shemya for fuel – all interesting wind-swept places!

As mentioned before, Tokyo was a great place to lay over so soon after the war. The roads were being upgraded as charcoal-burning cars were being phased out and modern autos were much in evidence. The staff house was a great rest stop with pleasant staff and great food and we got used to the early morning "honey buckets" being collected along our street.

Among our great stewardesses, Patsy S. was a Japanese Canadian who had been interned in Alberta with her parents during the war. On Tokyo layovers, she was a wonderful help with translation although the local people simply could not understand why she was unable to read or write Japanese when she spoke it so well.

In April, my second trip via Shemya met with a lengthy delay there after another aircraft taxied into our aircraft's tail! We spent several days in that cold wind-swept place while parts and personnel were flown in and repairs were effected, but our passengers were picked up by another carrier.

In the fall of 1957, I was transferred to the SAM (South American) route, flying to Mexico City and Lima, Peru. Upon leaving Mexico City with its high (7,300 foot) airport altitude, our take-off weight was severely restricted and we had to land at another airport for fuel – Houston or El Paso, Texas northbound and Acapulco, Tampico or Talara, Peru southbound. We enjoyed Mexico City with its wide streets and peso cabs which took us in a straight line from one end of the city to the other for just one peso (8 cents). Carrying no navigator, we were taught to use basic astro navigation between Mexico City and Lima.

On one flight, our crew had a day's layover in Mexico City. It was a fine day and our captain talked the base engineer into driving us to Lake Tequesquitengo for some water skiing. Taking some sandwiches and drinks, we pulled his boat down to the lake and after a few falls, I enjoyed my first time on skis. We later learned that the lake was quite contaminated!

On another flight – northbound from Lima – we co-pilots were detailed to look after our cargo of penguins which CPA was carrying from Santiago, Chile to Vancouver for Allan Best, the curator of the Stanley

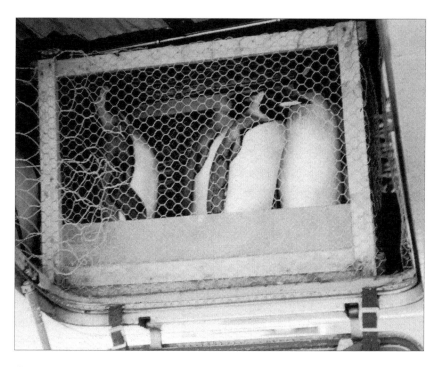

Our cargo of penguins at Lima, Peru needed exercising on the tarmac – one of the finest examples of the ever-changing jobs of a co-pilot!

Park Zoo. At each stop, we co-pilots were required to "walk" our charges up and down the tarmac. I believe we "lost" only two penguins from the 26 we carried.

While I had been in Ontario for our first son's birth, I was hoping I would not be in South America at year's end when our second baby was due. Indeed, I left for Lima on December 22nd, returned on the 29th and drove Joy to the hospital the very next day! And the Marpole Swing Bridge let us off the island for Joy's delivery, so the lengthy detour was not required!

I had been anticipating a promotion to captaincy flying DC-3s or Curtis C46 Commandos on Canada's Arctic DEW Line after my first year with CPA. However after the resupply contract was awarded to another carrier, instead of a promotion, my "Christmas present" at the end of my first year was a notice of layoff! I thus gladly accepted the company's new position of Simulator Instructor.

CPA's DC-6 cockpit simulator had been installed in one of their hangars which it later shared with its new Bristol Britannia simulator. Both were immovably bolted to the floor but had all the buttons, switches, sounds and control forces of the real aeroplane – and both were equipped with banks and banks of Russian-made and temperamental vacuum tubes, which kept the maintenance people very busy indeed.

Simulators are excellent training tools both for new pilots on that aircraft type and also for training on emergency procedures, and we trained CPA pilots to a very high standard. While our World War Two pilots had truly excellent "stick handling skills," I soon discovered that many were woefully lacking in their instrument flying skills and had to be coaxed into accepting additional training on the basics, until they became proficient at handling emergencies such as engine and cargo fires, as well as aircraft handling with two engines shut down on one side while flying blind.

While these initial simulators replaced the old Link Trainer, presented very realistic flying (all at night), saved the company a lot of money and freed up an aircraft for line flying, they were not considered a substitute for the actual aircraft when it came to proficiency checks. Pilots were still required to demonstrate their prowess in instrument flying and in handling a real DC-6 every six months.

On February 22nd, I climbed into our DC-6 simulator with a CPA line captain and demonstrated our simulator's capabilities to CPA's Chairman N. R. Crump, and then some days later to the camera crew of CBUT-TV. Other than the occasional light aeroplane flying and my semi-annual instrument rating flight, the simulator was my "airborne home" for a full year as I instructed or acted as pilot or co-pilot for first officers and captains in many different situations and different emergencies.

While CPA captains were very experienced pilots, many of them had not had much exposure to instrument flying. One of our jobs was to give them more practice at flying blind and we set to work. One captain, working his way through a lesson plan, was feeling a great deal of stress. To ease this, we broke off his lesson with an offer of coffee and opened his cockpit window, revealing the hangar wall right in front of him. This scared him absolutely silly and we all took an early coffee break!

Canadian Pacific Airlines called on me from time to time to assist in completing air tests and I flew every six months to demonstrate my abilities in the *real thing* to keep my Instrument Rating and Airline Transport Licence valid. I also underwent a medical examination every six months and kept my shots up to date. In addition, "just in case," I also renewed my Instructor's Rating with the Aero Club in one of their aircraft as a backup employment plan.

Our friendly Department of Transport annually required us to demonstrate a simulated ditching procedure which we carried out either in a swimming pool or, if weather permitted, on Vancouver's English Bay, using the life rafts and equipment from one of the DC-6s while it was in for maintenance. It was rather fun and the emergency candies from the survival rations were quite good, but we were all very glad when the launch finally arrived to pick us up.

In February 1959, I returned to full flying status on the familiar South American route to Lima, Peru as well as taking the odd trip on the SOPAC (South Pacific) run to Honolulu, Canton Island, Nadi (Fiji) and Auckland. I also flew a few extensions on to Sydney to relieve the Auckland-based crew which kept me away from home for several weeks.

Flying southbound from Honolulu was always an exciting time penetrating the ITZ (Intertropical Convergence Zone), a long line of thunderstorms that often barred the way to the South Pacific. While CPA had some newer DC-6s which were equipped with radar, these were flown by the senior pilots who chose to fly the Amsterdam route.

And so, on the Pacific route at either 15,000 or 16,000 feet, we flew quite blindly into that black wall of tropical thunderstorms. As we later learned, those black clouds sometimes rose to 50,000 feet and always promised those who entered them a rough ride. I remember hearing about an English B57 Canberra bomber which flew above a South

Pacific thunderstorm at an unbelievable 55,000 feet, had an upset and fell through the storm centre. Although able to land, the aircraft was then a total write-off.

Approaching the ITZ's black wall, electrical static cut off all radio contact. Ensuring that everyone and everything had been tied down securely, we headed into it. In the inky blackness amidst the constant drumming of heavy rain and frequent brilliant flashes of lightning which sometimes struck our aircraft, we were unable to see the green areas marking the hail. Then the constant roar of large hailstones pounding our thin aluminum skin and the frequent crash of thunder completely obliterated our engine noise and made verbal communications quite impossible while the almost constant turbulence made flying a straight course and altitude equally problematic. The blue electrical display (St. Elmo's Fire) around our propeller arcs often also covered our windshields and played havoc with our engine instruments, driving them absolutely crazy!

We occasionally saw static electricity forming a *ball of fire* on the nose of our aircraft which generally just exploded there with a tremendous "whump!" But on rare occasions, it entered the cockpit, emerged through our instrument panel and exploded inside the aircraft. On one occasion, during a brief lull in the turbulence, a ball of fire entered through the instrument panel, revolved over the throttle quadrant, dropped to the floor and rolled slowly down the aisle past our wide-eyed navigator and then on toward a stewardess who had just opened the cockpit door! She shrieked and ran aft with the ball *rolling along* behind her. Reports said that she ran into one of the two aft lavs while the ball chose the other, and once again, a loud "whump" signalled its departure!

Our static wicks, used to bleed static electricity from wings and tail, always took an awful beating on those flights and had to be replaced in Auckland. And occasionally, as the leading edges of our wings and tail took such a pounding from the heavy hailstones, they too had to be replaced.

A few moments after we had broken out on the south side of the ITZ, we would cautiously ask the navigator (sometimes two of them) our position. He had been bouncing around in his chair for 30 or 40 minutes, trying to keep track of the times spent on our various southerly headings as we dodged about. However after a few moments and a confirming "sun shot" (if available), he would point to a spot on his chart where his calculations told him we were and give us a revised heading.

On the south side of the ITZ, depending on winds and passenger loads, we sometimes had to land for fuel on one of two small atolls and it was therefore crucial to identify its radio beacon through the still-present but diminishing radio static. Almost always, we were able to land at Canton (Kanton) Island. Its runway had been built during WW2 on the largest most northerly atoll of the Phoenix Group of islands, just south of the equator and roughly halfway between Hawaii and Fiji, and we were always happy to "find" it as our fuel ran low.

Our second refuelling stop at Nadi, Fiji was a fun time for the happy locals as our passengers were offered fresh tropical drinks by the Fijians who pointed out the available *outhouse* facilities nearby. This provided much hilarity for the Fijians as they peeked through the outhouse knot-holes at the inmates!

Occupying the centre seat between the pilots after our take-off north-bound from Nadi one day, I was as appalled as were both our other two pilots at our slow climb in the hot air. We seemed to be almost brushing the wave tops for some distance until I suddenly noticed that the two pilots flying had forgotten to close the cowl flaps for take-off! I quietly reached forward and closed them to "trail" position and we commenced our climb, after which no one spoke for several minutes.

October 1959 found me back on the SAM (South American) route. While giving our Lima-based crew a holiday, several trips took me all the way to Buenos Aires via Santiago, Chile. Between Santiago and Buenos Aires, we climbed to 23,000 feet eastbound (24,000 feet westbound) and flew alongside majestic Mt. Aconcagua, South America's highest peak. Even at these altitudes, we were low enough to make out the struggling people on the tortuous road below.

On one dark night northbound from Lima, the captain pointed to

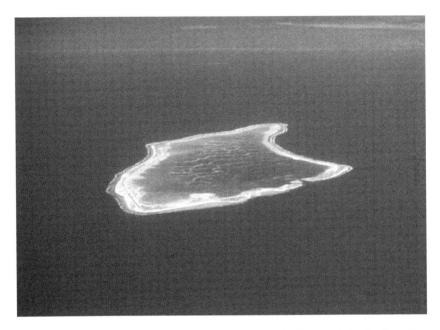

Canton Island, an occasional but much-needed refueling oasis in the broad Pacific's desert. Look closely to see the airstrip at the lower left of the atoll.

what appeared to be a black airship flying with us on his left-hand side. While difficult to judge distance, it was perhaps two hundred yards away and showed what appeared to be a dim row of lights running its entire length. It kept pace with us for what seemed like several minutes before climbing rapidly away to the west. It didn't seem to have any hot exhaust and our engines drowned out any noise it may have made. While the captain made an entry in the ship's log book, several UFO's had been sighted that year and we didn't really take more than a passing interest in it.

In early 1960 I was "downgraded" once again and assigned to fly the DC-6 on domestic flights, although I was "on call" and flew an occasional trip to Amsterdam. On this northern run over central Greenland, I enjoyed flying with senior captains who were flying the newer DC-6s equipped with *weather radar!* It was fascinating to watch the land go by without seeing it but it was rather a waste as far as weather was concerned, for there is very little thunderstorm activity on the Polar Run.

Domestic routes in BC were certainly not the best place for flying large four-engined aircraft, although our BC mountain runs made for some interesting flying with our experienced mountain crews. While CPA was a "scheduled airline," it was quite impossible to keep to any sort of a schedule during low cloud conditions in the mountains. The southern run from Vancouver to Penticton, Kelowna, Castlegar and Cranbrook to Calgary in conditions of low cloud forced the crews to fly through the valleys between the mountains so that IFR (Instrument Flight Rules) came to mean "I Follow Roads". And more than one pilot carried a road map along in his back pocket as a handy navigational reference.

As the aircraft left each airport, its passenger agent phoned ahead to the next station so that waiting passengers could be advised as to the time we could be expected. On one such a day, we took off from Castlegar toward the north and levelled off at about 400 feet beneath the low clouds. Around the hill, as we turned eastward towards Cranbrook, we came head to head with a Republic Seabee flying at our altitude! Following the rules, we both immediately banked to the right, thereby avoiding a nasty collision!

That winter, an icy runway in Prince George coupled with a strong crosswind had us skidding about and we ended up rolling tail first down the runway, forcing us to *advance* the throttles to stop at the end of the runway!

One of the DC-6s (probably CF-CUO) I had flown was later blown out of the skies near 100 Mile House in July 1965 by an explosive device placed in one of its lavatories, killing all 46 passengers and 6 crew. I never asked who the crew was, but it gave us all some food for thought.

As the DC-6 was being withdrawn from domestic routes, in January 1961 I was trained to fly the smaller Convair 240 which had just two engines, two pilots and one stewardess and carried 40 passengers. Hot air from the engines was ducted to the wings and tail for anti-icing and while the wings were kept clear, the hot air had cooled by the time it reached the tail.

Flying in cloud one day northbound above the Fraser Canyon with ice building on our tail, we were unable to maintain altitude and descended slowly under its increasing weight. We were well below our minimum safe altitude when we thankfully broke out of cloud between the hills approaching Ashcroft and we turned and landed at Kamloops. There, we and our passengers waited patiently as 4 inches of ice slowly melted from the leading edges of our tail before leaving for Prince George.

However the Convair was much more manoeuvrable than the DC-6 and we enjoyed flying into such places as the downtown airstrip at Cranbrook over their local lumber yard. I took Joy for a ride on our mountain run one day and she was occupying the observer's seat behind the pilot as we banked around Old Glory Mountain and "scared the dickens out of the chickens!"

As our flight from Penticton to Kelowna was scheduled during the noon dinnertime, CPA boarded a second stewardess and the two were required to serve hot meals to our (up to) 40 passengers during the 12-minute flight! Salad trays were distributed to passengers as they boarded, a small hot dinner was served immediately as we became air-borne and the stewardesses kept begging us to do another circuit over Kelowna so passengers could gulp down their desserts. Trays were then collected from our grateful passengers as they disembarked! We might have been late, but at least our passengers were fed.

In June 1961 I had returned to flying the DC-6 when David, our third son and a beautiful baby, came into this world. Joy waved him at her "three boys" below on the hospital lawn for we were not allowed to bring children into the hospital wards. Our two boys were thrilled with their new baby brother and immediately began "teaching him."

Joy's niece came to live with us that fall so she could complete her last year of high school. While our house was then quite full, she became our built-in babysitter which allowed us to have the odd evening out.

Frequent layoff threats were made, even as my seniority climbed from #272 to #170 in 5 years. Towards the end of 1961, CPA Captain Jimmy McGuire offered me a job flying as a captain on one of CPA's DC-6s which was to be leased to a Yellowknife charter company known as "Wardair" and would be based in Edmonton. At a starting salary of $500 per month, I accepted his offer, so my last flight with CPA (Edmonton to Prince George) occurred on January 13th of 1962.

WARDAIR DC-6

Leaving Joy with her niece for company, I assisted Art Gauthier, a CPA navigator who was then busy selling Wardair charter flights to England on an aircraft we did not yet have! CF-CZZ was a convertible DC-6C passenger/freighter which was lease-purchased by Wardair for one year and came equipped with radar. My log book shows a total of 6,232 hours of flying, 2,267 of which were in DC-6s when I became the first pilot hired by Wardair for its Edmonton operation.

On March 14th, I flew in CZZ to Edmonton together with three skilled CPA mechanics to look after it. Along with our load of spare aircraft parts, our brand new red Volvo 122S was tucked away safely inside together with the piled up passenger seats, thus craftily avoiding paying the BC sales tax! Our Volvo purchase price at the time was an even $2,000 plus $58 for the radio.

In Edmonton I met Maxwell W. "Max" Ward, the WW2 and Yellowknife bush pilot who was just then entering Canada's international charter field. I soon discovered that charter flying was quite different from scheduled flying and it opened up real challenges for organization and innovation. For example, I designed our pilot's uniforms for freighting operations based on the RCAF's battle dress uniforms. It should be mentioned that several great CPA navigators and mechanics also flew with Wardair and many remained with the company.

We were required to research the airports from which we were to operate, complete with let-down charts (obtained from Jeppesen), runway lengths, load restrictions, fuel availability, ground handling equipment and loading personnel, etc. Crew accommodation, meals and transportation at various airports had also to be considered. To help matters somewhat, I had discovered that we could legally raise our maximum landing weight by 5% when flying in freighter configuration, and this news pleased Max no end! Charter flying was indeed a whole new world.

It seemed strange flying from the Edmonton airport again in 1962, this time operating from the terminal on the west side, but all fell into place following my semi-annual instrument check on March 14th with CZZ now in freighter configuration. As I had never flown as captain on the DC-6, the following day I flew with Harry March, Wardair's first captain and chief pilot, via Wardair's Yellowknife base to our main freighting base of Resolute Bay.

Resolute Bay on Cornwallis Island was a windy, snowy, Arctic air base which was operated by the RCAF and supplied by ship each summer. Supplies were then distributed by air to various Arctic outposts when weather permitted. Our photo of Resolute, taken on April 23,1953, shows a Lancaster photo reconnaissance aircraft through the blowing snow.

The RCAF in Resolute Bay kindly accommodated us (in triple bunks) and fed us. It became our refuelling base and from there our cargo, left by the previous summer's resupply ship, was loaded. Our initial job was to fly many tons of supplies to the high Arctic islands of Isachsen on Ellef Ringnes Island, Mould Bay on Prince Patrick Island and Eureka Sound on Ellesmere Island.

Resolute Bay often spray-painted its snow-covered centre runway markings in red for better landing visibility. In high wind conditions, this gradually blew off and it was not uncommon to read weather conditions at Resolute as "winds northeast at 30, visibility 2 miles in pink drifting snow" (PDS).

In the Air Force, I had been made aware of the danger when refuelling aircraft while wearing nylon parkas, for sparks from static electricity

Above: *This is what Resolute Bay, our northern re-supply aerodrome, often looked like each spring! This photo, taken in 1953 when I was with the RCAF, shows an RCAF Avro Lancaster bomber through the blowing snow.*

could be seen showering down from them in the dark Arctic air. I therefore requested and received cotton parkas and we wore them while on top of the wing and, along with the caution required while walking along the frosty wings, we took extra precautions during refuelling operations.

Our cargo consisted mostly of about 70 drums of fuel oil, each weighing between 430 and 455 pounds. Our "reserve pilot" dug these barrels out of the hard-packed snow with a forklift during the long Resolute nights, loaded them into the aircraft and tied them down. Our DC-6 cargo area was left unheated and barrels were left in their frozen state. Our crew consisted of three pilots, a mechanic and a loadmaster. No navigators were carried and, as we operated within an area where compasses were useless, pilots used a grid navigation system developed by our CPA navigator Ed Parliament called "Parliament's Patented Polar Plot."

Don Holinaty, our super-strong loader (and un-loader) handles fuel oil barrels weighing more than 400 pounds with ease. His aim was always right on the mark! Singing the wartime tune "Roll Out the Barrels," they came tumbling out!

Upon arrival at our destination, engines one, two and three were shut down and, while one pilot was left in the cockpit to "mind the shop," everyone else donned parkas and rushed aft. The big cargo door was opened, the barrel chute that Max had designed was deployed and barrels started rolling. Our record was 72 barrels offloaded in just 7 minutes, from the time the aircraft stopped rolling at Isachsen until we started to roll again! We took full advantage of the longer daylight hours, for I logged 117 flying hours in just two weeks while completing two and sometimes three round trips each day into Canada's high Arctic.

On April 3rd, we were just completing our flight to Mould Bay when a call came that we were needed in Ottawa. After refuelling in Resolute, we flew to Ottawa where a helicopter was loaded for Cape Dyer on the Arctic Circle at the eastern tip of Baffin Island. Max Ward himself supervised its delicate unloading in the strong gusty winds.

On April 9th, after completing several trips from Resolute, CPA called asking us to take an engine from Vancouver to Honolulu as its aircraft was stuck there with an engine problem. After refuelling in Resolute, we flew to Yellowknife for a quick rest in the staff house. Next day we flew to Fort Smith, to Edmonton, then to Vancouver for the new engine (and our wives!), and finally to Honolulu, a flight which took 11 hours 23 minutes. Our total flying time from Yellowknife to Honolulu was 17 hours. Dead tired, I collapsed on the beach with Joy who was unable to wake me and we both became thoroughly sunburnt! Three days later, we returned our wives and the unserviceable engine to Vancouver and then flew back to Yellowknife.

On April 18th, after one trip to Inuvik and having checked the ice thickness on Contwoyto Lake (about halfway between Yellowknife and Bathurst Inlet), we began flying freight from Yellowknife to Contwoyto where we discovered that cold ice was just as good as cement to land on. I logged 135 hours in April and in May. I made seven more trips to Contwoyto Lake and one east to Montreal before returning to Edmonton.

In Edmonton, our DC-6 became a passenger aircraft once more, outfitted with 88 seats, carpeted floors, a complete galley and two lava-tories! Max asked me to recommend a chief stewardess for flying with passengers and I highly recommended Maryanne Wynnychuk, a girl who had been flying with me in CPA. Maryanne agreed, designed a Wardair uniform, drew up menus, organized passenger amenities and hired a couple of her compatriots to help crew Wardair's first passenger flight, the Calgary School Safety Patrol, to Ottawa and back. I then enjoyed two whole weeks off for a visit with my family and planning our move.

Even while working flat out, I thoroughly missed my family and we agreed to another move, renting a split level house on the west side of Edmonton. Joy's niece was finishing her school year and our real estate agent was able to sell our Richmond house (for $12,500). Our Ford sold to a friend, Joy arranged with the movers, then flew with our three boys to Edmonton. Following a brief visit to Sylvan Lake, we cleaned the rented house, the furniture arrived, and we moved in at the beginning of June. Although Joy started a garden, she was very disappointed with Edmonton's short growing season and the relatively poor quality of the soil compared to Richmond.

Following one more trip to Resolute Bay with freight, our aircraft was once more made ready for passengers – for overseas flights. For these long flights, the flight crew protested that no crew rest facilities were provided – "it would be awfully nice to be able to stretch out when not on duty." Max quite agreed and had the galley moved aft two feet so triple bunks (24" x 24" x 6') could be installed in the available space. While these "coffins" were located between the four noisy propellers, no one complained and crews became quite experienced listening from their cubby-holes as the operating pilots "thermal shocked" the engines one at a time each hour with a rich fuel mixture and primer fuel to clean the cylinders.

In preparations for our first overseas flight, Joy was asked to purchase the terribly-important yet nearly-forgotten alcoholic drinks for our passengers. She picked up a selection of different spirits at the local vendor which filled a large grocery buggy and was then asked if she had a banquet permit for it! She believes the total came to $88 (remember this was back in 1962).

Pilots completed their own weight and balance calculations using DOT (Department of Transport) approved standard passenger weights. These were 165 pounds for males and 143 pounds for females which included coats, briefcases, purses, umbrellas, etc. I frequently thought about our actual take-off weights as we prepared for longer trips with some pretty hefty-looking passengers. In succeeding years, only one station that we flew to required all passengers to be weighed along with their baggage prior to boarding, and we were confident that we were always "legal" leaving Belfast!

Charter rules of the day stipulated that we could only operate "affinity flights," meaning that all our passengers had to belong to the same organization for at least six months. On June 22nd, 1962, all was in readiness for our first overseas flight. Inside our DC-6 to check that our

88 passengers were indeed *bona fide* members of their society was a government inspector while outside, at the foot of the stairs in the bright summer sunshine, was a smartly-dressed stewardess who welcomed them all on board – and issued back-dated membership cards for those still unequipped.

Flying via the "polar route" (a great circle route) to Europe took us to Frobisher Bay (the airfield was built by the US in 1942) now known as Iqaluit, Nunavut on Baffin Island, then to Prestwick, Scotland for more fuel and finally to our destination of Copenhagen, Denmark with a flying time of 18 hours 18 minutes and a *duty day* of 22 hours! On our empty return trip which took 17 hours 40 minutes, we refuelled at the Sondrestrom Airbase, located at the end of a long fjord just north of the Arctic Circle in Western Greenland. This American airbase, used also by Scandinavian Airlines (SAS), was at one time called "Bluie West 8" and is now known as "Kangerlussuak." We simply called it "Sondy."

Our second flight to Copenhagen was routed via Goose Bay, Labrador (due to the wind pattern) and we returned via Frobisher Bay on June 29th showing a round trip flying time of 36 hours 28 minutes. This was my final captain's check ride and from then on, it was *CAPTAIN* Gartshore who received a fourth uniform stripe and doubled his income as he assumed responsibility for every decision made on his flight. In subsequent years, I was occasionally asked to perform a wedding, but unlike a ship's captain, I was never licensed to do so.

Besides Copenhagen that summer, we carried people to London's Heathrow Airport, Prestwick in Scotland and Shannon in Ireland from either Edmonton or Toronto. Prior to returning to Edmonton at night from Toronto on August 20th, Maryanne gave a quick course to Anne, my future sister-in-law, who then helped her operate our domestic flight to Edmonton. My brother also came along on this trip as a passenger!

Our first summer was not only passenger work. With the aircraft returned to its freighter configuration the following day (August 22nd) and with two complete flying crews, #1 crew with Harry March flew us to Saskatoon, Yellowknife and Resolute Bay. My crew (#2) then operated

Sondrestrom, Greenland. Behind the mileage post, one of Wardair's first arrivals in 1962 takes on fuel while passengers "take on" souvenirs.

from Resolute to Mould Bay, back to Resolute, to Isachsen, then back to Resolute. Crew #1 carried us to Alert (the world's most northerly airport at the foot of mountains reaching up to 8,500 feet) and Thule, Greenland, then our crew flew back to Alert, Thule, Alert, Resolute, Mould Bay and Resolute. Crew #1 then flew us down to Calgary where we took over again and flew us all back to Edmonton on August 29th! Isn't it amazing what long daylight hours will allow workers to accomplish? I flew a total of 124 hours and 20 passenger hours in August.

Joy brought our three boys to the airport to welcome me home and Marjorie Ward also brought her family with her. Our almost-five-year-old son Brian was overawed as the big DC-6 was slowly pushed back into its small hangar with just inches to spare. Dancing up and down with excitement, he boasted to the boy beside him that, "My daddy flies that plane!" until the other finally retorted, "Well, my daddy *owns* that plane!"

That fall, after a passenger charter to London, I flew a flurry of charters to such diverse places as Tampico, Mexico; Houston, Texas; Oklahoma City and Great Falls, Montana. With time on our hands as the charter business fell off, we operated as a "polishing crew" to polish the DC-6 and Max polished his 4x6 foot section of aluminum right next to mine. The decision was reluctantly taken to return our leased DC-6 to Vancouver at the beginning of November and after a farewell BBQ at the Wards, once again and to my chagrin, I was placed on laid-off status.

With a wife and three boys to feed, I found a job with Federated Growth (which later became Dynamic Funds), selling little-known "mutual funds" to business owners up and down Kingsway Avenue during Edmonton's bitterly cold winter of 1962-63. I was surprisingly successful at selling mutual funds!

In March of 1963, Wardair leased a DC-6A freighter (CF-CZQ) from CPA. I was returned from laid-off status to full-time flying and we headed north once again. CZQ could carry more freight than CZZ for it carried no passenger amenities while maximum take-off and landing weights remained the same. It was amazing that we were able to complete so many trips with so few cancellations due to weather, although we were forced to return occasionally due to gusty cross-winds without unloading. Maximum cross-winds of 26 knots were not uncommon as each Arctic site had but one snow-covered airstrip. These strips were not at all slippery at cold temperatures and we enjoyed the satisfaction of a soft touchdown on the snow-drifted runways.

With such a top notch maintenance crew, we were almost free from mechanical problems, but on April 5th I was forced to turn back to Resolute Bay when an engine became increasingly cranky. While we throttled it back and babied it, following an examination in Resolute it was declared to be "unserviceable." We made the best of our Resolute stay as mechanics changed the engine with one brought up from Edmonton, but it was three full days in the long daylight hours before we were able to resume our cargo flights to Mould Bay.

On one of our many trips to Isachsen, a full load of dynamite had been loaded on board and then, at the last minute, we were asked if we

Above: *In 1963, Wardair's leased DC-6 (CF-CZQ) unloads freight at Mould Bay in the bright spring sunshine. The barrel ramp device designed and built by Wardair's boss expedited our unloading. Wardair's northern re-supply contract was instrumental in starting the fledgling airline.*

Below: *Mould Bay in the spring of 1963, loading freight.*

would carry some mail. We were, of course, always happy to do this for our isolated Arctic posts and some packages were duly tied down on top of the dynamite and the cargo door closed. It was a good thing we landed gently at Isachsen, for the "mail packages" turned out to be the blasting caps for the tons of dynamite tied down just below it!

For several days we flew building materials and other supplies onto Speers Lake, a small lake just north of the Arctic Circle near the Coppermine River, in support of Canada's Polar Continental Shelf Project. An advance party had arrived in a Wardair Otter to measure the ice thickness at various points along the ice over our freshwater landing area. After making sure we had sufficient ice to take our DC-6 landing weight of 92,000 pounds, Wardair's Bristol Freighter landed a D4 Caterpillar Tractor which cleared the snow from a 5,000-foot-long strip of ice. The ice must have been thick enough, for on our many trips, we never fell through!

Most days had low overcast clouds so we had the cooks direct us overhead their shack on their VHF radio, from which point we calculated our cloud-breaking approach. Then it was back to the Arctic! My log book shows *152:14 hours* of flying in April and on our last trip, I was given a full barrel of fresh Arctic char by the great Resolute Bay staff to take with us to Edmonton for a crew celebration. However I was simply so tired that I forgot all about it and it became just a mouldy stink in the hangar. Yuck!

I was often so tired after a series of flights that my head was buzzing. I would come home, usually in the evening, say hello to my family, then relax into an easy chair. Plugging my ears into a stack of records playing Mozart or Bach, I would turn up the volume and enter a deep sleep which gradually eased the throbbing of the engines and I would then crawl into bed.

Joy was a very lonely girl during those long periods that I was away working such long hours. The boys took up much of her time, of course, but it was a difficult period in her life. She was a trained Red Cross Water

Safety Course Instructor and for several years taught adult swimming at the local Strathcona Pool.

At the beginning of May, Wardair took delivery of its first *purchased* DC-6. It was an older passenger-only model (DC-6B) which came from KLM Royal Dutch Airlines and had no radar. A further drawback was that all its emergency equipment instructions were in Dutch and we had very few Dutch speaking crew members! We were truly very happy therefore that, upon completing our flying with this aircraft two years later, we had not been required to use any of its emergency equipment. But on the positive side, as a passenger aircraft it had an honest-to-goodness crew bunk above the front end passengers.

Max explained that since we now "owned" this aircraft, we were required to produce an operating manual to satisfy the Ministry of Transport, so I cobbled one together, freely using CPA's manual but without its fancy drawings.

In May, my first trip with our new DC-6, with Canadian registration of CF-PCI, took us from Calgary via Sondrestrom to London's Heathrow Airport and Amsterdam. The following morning we were bussed down to London's Gatwick Airport and returned to Edmonton via Rotterdam and Keflavik Iceland. All charter operations thereafter were routed to and from the Gatwick airport.

In mid-May 1963, we made a few more trips from Yellowknife with CF-CZQ, our leased CPA freighter, to complete the contract at Contwoyto and Speers Lakes. On one of our trips into Yellowknife, we spotted a large twin-engine flying boat sporting the familiar Wardair colours at the dock which, on closer inspection, turned out to be a very rare Supermarine Stranraer, a 1930s British-built flying boat biplane (two wings) which Wardair had leased for the summer to carry lumber into the Arctic. Due to its box-like fuselage, it was able to carry more lumber than its more modern Catalina cousin. Although we enjoyed sitting in its cockpit, I regretfully relate that I was not one of the very few Wardair pilots who flew it.

While I cannot be certain, I believe it was on June 19th, after flying

In 1963, the crew of Wardair's very own DC-6 (CF-PCI) prepares to welcome our guests. Front row, from left – Don Saunders (co-pilot); Walt Lowe (navigator). Second row – Bob Gartshore (captain). Third row – Bob Hemsley (co-pilot); Ed Parliament (navigator). Fourth row – Brenda Mallen (stewardess); Maryanne McIndoe (nee Wynnychuk) (chief stewardess). Fifth/top row – Pat Brault (stewardess); Helen Maclagan (stewardess).

CZQ from Resolute Bay to Isachsen to Mould Bay to Isachsen and back to Resolute that it was in Isachsen that we loaded a badly-damaged Bell 47 helicopter. En route to Calgary, its pilot told us his story. With no night that far north, it seems that "Red" (who had red hair) had been camped out on the ice north of Isachsen and was sleeping quite peacefully when he heard a noise outside his tent.

Before he was fully awake, a polar bear tore Red's tent away! Without time to reach the Very Pistol (flare gun) inside his sleeping bag, Red landed his clenched fist on the bear's nose, whereupon the bear backed off with blood spurting from it. Red was then able to extract his pistol and fire a flare at the bear which ambled off. However his helicopter had been pretty well trashed as we confirmed when having a better look at it as we flew southward.

In mid-June, we began flying our Edmonton and Calgary passengers to Europe in earnest, dropping them off in Copenhagen, Oslo, London Gatwick, Amsterdam and Manchester. While we normally stopped for fuel at Frobisher, Sondrestrom or Keflavik, our empty flight from Oslo on July 11th managed a non-stop flight back to Edmonton in just over *16 hours*!

One hot August day, just after reaching our 16,000-foot cruising altitude out of Sondrestrom, one engine showed that *both* spark plugs were not firing in one of its 18 cylinders. As this indicated possible cylinder damage, we shut it down, feathered the prop and returned to Sondy. All was well again after both spark plugs were replaced. Feeling much relieved, we departed for Manchester two hours later. I logged 125 hours that month.

In September 1963, I flew north again in our re-leased CZZ for another spell of freighting. We were going at it hammer and tongs when, halfway through the month and on our third flight that day approaching Mould Bay in cloud, our radar showed us passing over the edge of the last hill and I insisted that we begin our descent into the valley through the cloud. Suddenly, the edge of that hill loomed out of the cloud ahead of us and, upon pulling up, our tail grazed it, putting operations back a month while extensive repairs were carried out.

I well remember walking up to the Mould Bay operations building to file our accident report accompanied by two very large wild Arctic wolves. I will be forever grateful that Max stood by me – said he had made mistakes too.

Our crew had logged more than 124 hours of flying time in the previous three weeks which made us all rather tired. After the aircraft was made flyable, it was ferried to Edmonton and my freighting career then ended for, after repairs were complete, we returned CZZ to CPA and thereafter all our DC-6 flying was done with PCI, our passenger aircraft.

One additional note on freighting must be added: We had been offered the grand sum of 50 cents a barrel to bring the empties out of the Arctic. This offer however was quite impractical, for even had we been offered ten times that sum, we had been working flat out and had no time to retrieve them.

In October, Wardair outfitted PCI with a second navigator's periscopic sextant station near the main entrance door. After a single passenger trip to London, a geo-magnetic survey crew came aboard in Ottawa and our 12-man crew headed north to Thule, Greenland. With two navigators working full time cross-checking our position, we began flying each night back and forth in long parallel flights 100 miles apart as far as Russian airspace. We used Canada's unique airborne magnetometer to check the location of the Earth's magnetic North Pole which was then moving northward. Each time we approached Russian airspace, Anchorage Air Traffic Control warned us that we were approaching "dangerous airspace" over which they had no control. We moved our base of operations from Thule to Resolute Bay and Max himself flew with us on some trips where he occasionally "put his hand to the tiller."

Then from Inuvik, our last base of operations, we flew directly over the geographic North Pole on November 5th! We operated several more trips until one engine became tired and we returned to Edmonton on three engines while #4 took a holiday, a flight which took over 13 hours.

I logged 141 hours and 40,000 miles in just 17 days that month, nearly all of it at night. I learned quite recently that the magnetic North Pole is moving faster than at any time in recorded history and is expected to be located on the Siberian side of the geographic North Pole by the year 2020!

At our European base of operations at London Gatwick, crews were put up at the nearby Ye Old Felbridge Inn. This pleasant rural inn was owned by a Mr. Gatward whose sons had a model train set up in the attic. There was a solar-heated swimming pool for the occasional summer swim. The inn's staff never seemed to mind whenever we arrived late or departed early and we came to enjoy our Gatwick base. I stored my three-speed bike in their shed and spent many happy hours getting to know the Crawley area. Joy and I spent a night in one of their rooms which couldn't be locked as it was one of the inn's *emergency escape routes.*

I was scheduled to fly an empty aircraft over to London one day when Bev, my co-pilot's wife, called Joy with the suggestion that she join her *that afternoon* for our flight to Gatwick and "a bike ride along southern England!"

"I don't have a babysitter," Joy protested.

"Get one," Bev said.

"I don't have a bike," Joy said.

"Buy one over there," came the order.

A grandmother just happened to be visiting her family next door and Joy talked her into looking after our three boys for three days while I flew over to England and back. And so it came about that the two girls flew over with us, Joy bought a Raleigh three-speed bike, and the girls set off on an adventure that found the English Downs to be mostly "Ups."

Although we were supposed to pick them up in Belfast two weeks later, I was taken off the flight at the last moment and the girls returned with our chief pilot occupying "my" seat! It was a rough flight on their way home and on her arrival at Canada Customs, poor Joy was asked if she had anything to declare. Looking quite green, she honestly replied,

Circumstances allowed two young mothers to seize the opportunity to tour southern England "on the cheap."

"I think I'm going to throw up," and thereupon was quickly ushered through customs!

There were some wonderful shopping bargains to be had in London and I was able to buy woollen goods there very reasonably. As my mother had always worn moss green, I came home with a lovely woollen suit for Joy in moss green which fit her perfectly. I was so pleased with myself that later that summer I found another and a skirt that also fit her perfectly. But before I brought home yet more, she confessed with tears in her eyes that she looked simply terrible in moss green! Indeed she had worn one beautiful moss green suit to church one Sunday and everyone told her that she should go home as she didn't look well. I restricted myself thereafter to buying jewels. They *always* fit.

One of the wonderful sights flight crews are privileged to witness occurs when either climbing slowly out of a cloud layer or just prior to entering one on descent. With the sun somewhere behind the aircraft, the shadow of our aircraft forms a visible cross ahead of us, known by pilots as the "airman's cross" and we recall the poem *High Flight* by John G. McGee (see last page).

Another great sight we witnessed time and time again during those long winter nights eastbound over northern Canada was the dancing curtains of colourful Northern Lights (Aurora Borealis) pulsating across the North's dark skies. These frequently sported an array of different colours rather than just the usual green glow. And on westbound flights approaching Greenland along the Arctic Circle, crews were privileged to view, from our 14,000 foot perch in the sky, the clutter of icebergs and the grandeur of the deep fjords with their lateral moraines splitting the east coast.

However, one of the most spectacular sights I have ever seen occurred during the eruption of an underwater volcano off the south coast of Iceland which began in November 1963 and lasted for several months. We first saw the eruption on December 5th while ferrying an empty aircraft back from Amsterdam. As we approached Keflavik, the new island of Surtsey had begun to take shape. The eruption cloud reached several thousand feet and could be seen from many miles away.

Cleared for the approach, we descended early and saw several explosions, occasional flashes of lighting and columns of steam as the sizzling falling bombs hit the ocean, sometimes half a mile away from the island. The eruption continued spasmodically and while no one had ventured onto the island to that point, a party of journalists landed on the island a few days after we left, despite the danger from falling bombs! We carried on to Edmonton where we arrived after our twelve-and-a-half-hour flight with one engine shut down – my third that year! I never heard if it had ingested ash from the Surtsey volcano, but we had not flown anywhere close to the cloud rising from the eruption.

My next flight to Iceland took place at the end of March 1964 by

Top: *The awe-inspiring, never-to-be-forgotten sight of one of the world's great natural volcanic occurrences forming Surtsey Island.*

Above: *A later flight, high over Surtsey. Bird life quickly came to the new island, well before human arrivals.*

which time a new eruption from the island was forming a lagoon containing floating pumice. The new island of Surtsey was now more than one square kilometre in area. By July, it was almost quiet.

While Edmonton winters were often bright and sunny, they were indeed cold and dark and downright miserable when cloudy. On one such day in February, Joy and I were shopping downtown and entered a pet store to get warm. Inside was a cute little black-and-white English bulldog-cross that we fell in love (and came home) with. The boys instantly fell in love with "Patty" and they spent many happy hours entertaining each other. When I was home on sunny weekends, I could bundle them all into the Volvo and drive to the hill overlooking the Saskatchewan River for some sleigh and cardboard riding, Patty running vociferously alongside!

Once again, winter flying contracts were slow and we were all given November off for our annual holidays. One of our pilots owned a small farm near Spruce Grove and Wardair was invited to gather there for hot chocolate and snowmobiling. Many of us, including Max and Marjorie, spent a hilarious day in the winter sunshine out on the rolling farmland with toboggans and a snowmobile.

While we very much enjoyed our three boys, Joy had always wanted a girl. She relates that when she was very young, she was told by her girl friend that the way to get a baby was to ask the doctor because "he makes them." So one very cold winter's morning, the two girls knocked on the good doctor's door and when he answered, Joy's friend told him that they wanted a baby. The gruff doctor said, "Well, you'll have to wait awhile" and closed the door. And so they sat down on his steps and waited. Finally a neighbour saw them waiting and told them to go home and *"wait until you are grown up!"*

The only way to guarantee a baby girl after having three boys seemed to be the adoption route and we began the lengthy process which culminated in receiving a tiny eight-month-old baby girl in the early spring of 1964. Brenda Helen adjusted quickly to being held and our boys (and

Patty) enjoyed her very much – David even kissing her bum as he carried her around head down and folded over his arms!

Our Sylvan Lake property had been sold to our minister by my parents, and in the summer we rented its guest cottage so our family could enjoy a month's holiday there. It was a bit of a squeeze getting our family of six, plus the dog, into the Volvo but we managed. Although electricity had been installed, Joy washed the diapers for a while by hand on a scrub board which, while it got them white after drying in the sun, was a great deal of work! We later found and purchased a tiny table-top washing machine for the diapers. As it was 5 miles to town by road, the family was quite dependent on my coming and going for its shopping and flying kept me very busy. I received my first (and so far only) speeding ticket while driving down to the cottage following an overseas flight and I hadn't been paying attention to my speed.

From time to time during my career, I crossed paths with George Hunter, who could arguably be one of Canada's greatest photographers. His photos have graced the Canadian 5, 10 and 50 dollar bills and he is noted for his work with the National Film Board. George and Max Ward got along well as both were pilots of the same age. Our crews (and aircraft) frequently posed for the advertising photographs George did for Wardair. I remember arriving at Montreal's Dorval airport and, as we taxied up to the terminal, being greeted by a great mound of photographic equipment, announcing George's next flight with us.

The summer of 1964 stood out for me as the season of airport variation. Ports of call showed a real variety: Oslo, Saskatoon, Zurich, Shannon, Aalberg, Whitehorse, Cologne, Copenhagen, Frankfurt, Prestwick, Goose Bay, Winnipeg, Manchester, Regina and Amsterdam. In July, I logged 133 flying hours. While this may not sound excessive from those working a normal 40 hours per week, it must be remembered that flight preparation, annual ditching drills, periodic written exams, simulator exercises, ongoing flight manual updates, medical exams, crew positioning and other such activities are indeed "extras" and most pilots today are limited to just 85 hours of "working air time" per month.

One hot summer day in Saskatoon, while our aircraft was being cleaned and refuelled, Don Holinaty, our burly aircraft loader, became forever famous when he opened the lavatory drain valve below the tail of the aircraft before completely securing the drain hose. Seconds later, in a very loud voice heard all around the airport, he uttered the apt and most memorable words, "OH SHIT!"

One of our pilots, whose father owned an Edmonton funeral home, loved regaling us with tales of deceased persons. He owned a two-seat aircraft which his father often chartered to transport corpses to Edmonton and was flying a recently deceased passenger down from Yellowknife one day as rigour mortis was setting in. His "passenger" on the seat beside him insisted on pressing down on one of the rudder pedals on his side of the aircraft, "helping" him to steer!

Dreaming of "our own home," we purchased a divided VLA (Veteran's Land Act) 1/4-acre lot near Edmonton's Southgate Centre for $4,000. I drafted up a two-storey house with a split level entry and found a builder who was willing to start work that September. The construction was to cost $22,000. His crew was just finishing the interior painting on December 23rd when we moved in. By the time my mother arrived from Vancouver the following day, all was in readiness for Christmas. Joy has always been super efficient.

We began taking passengers to Honolulu in mid-February of 1965 and our flights to and from Alberta landed at either San Francisco or Portland for fuel. Edmonton to San Francisco took 5 hours and San Francisco to Honolulu took 10. On one of our return flights from Honolulu, we listened attentively to the radio as a Pan American Stratocruiser limped back to Honolulu having suffered the loss of two engines on one side of the aircraft. It was forced to fly at wave top level where it was assisted by ground effect but was in danger of ditching at any moment. I certainly appreciated those geese at the lake when I was a kid, showing off how ground effect could assist them! We eventually went out of radio contact, but assume it landed safely for we heard no report of its ditching.

I was scheduled to fly an empty aircraft to Honolulu on March 25th, and then fly a load of passengers home three days later. It was a perfect opportunity to take my family for a quick vacation. On the evening of the 25th, I checked my family in and went upstairs to the weather office with our navigator. On return, I found everyone looking for our seven-year-old son Brian who had disappeared! With visions of a delayed flight before us, the search became quite frantic until we boarded PCI to do our pre-flight inspection and discovered that Brian had pre-boarded himself and was in one of the rear seats sound asleep. Our non-stop flight thereafter took an uneventful 12-1/2 hours and yes, we all enjoyed our beach time.

I sometimes wondered when we took off from Honolulu with our load of passengers just how we would make out if we experienced an engine failure. While the runway was certainly long enough for take-off at our maximum gross weight of 107,000 pounds, we were "temperature limited" and occasionally had to wait until the air temperature cooled sufficiently to allow a legal departure with the fuel on board, or remove 72 pounds of fuel for every degree the air temperature was over the standard 59°F. I can assure you that we watched the engine gauges quite closely as Diamond Head swept majestically by the cockpit windows at our altitude!

Later that year, Max was negotiating with Boeing on the purchase of a jet aircraft and to save money, we agreed to operate with just the minimum required maintenance. On one of our westbound trips in April, due to a Canadian ATC (Air Traffic Control) strike, we had flown from Sondrestrom to Whitehorse for fuel and were proceeding down to Edmonton when we were forced to shut down a tired engine (why was it always an outboard engine?) and landed there on three.

We enjoyed our flights across Greenland and when we occasionally spotted the American DEW Line radar stations of "Sea Bass" and "Sob Story" situated high atop the icecap along the Arctic Circle, we talked to their crews to relieve the boredom they must have felt. There were also radar sites on both coasts, one near Holsteinborg on the west coast and one on Kalusuk Island on the beautiful east coast near Angmagssalik known as "Big Gun."

Our family had enjoyed their cottage stay so much that in 1965 we took a ten-year lease on it and drove down for the summer. During my days off, I installed a propane stove as the wood stove made the cabin so hot. We also bought a great looking 1962 Chevrolet BelAir four-door hardtop which enabled Joy to shop and do our laundry in town. It was not only a relief for her to be independent but also eased her mind to have "wheels" in the event of an emergency.

When I came home after a trip, I was kept busy with house maintenance but still found time for shopping (which Joy hates!) before driving down to the cottage. The Woodward's Store in Southgate was an amazing place to shop, for I tore through their women's and children's departments on sale days selecting clothing I thought would interest Joy. The clerks put it all in a large cardboard box which I took down to the cottage. After Joy had made her selection, I returned the rest to the store. It was indeed a happy time.

My worst ever nightmare occurred on an otherwise fine July day in 1965 while flying with an ex-CPA captain. Approaching Frobisher Bay, we decided to carry on to Sondrestrom as its forecast remained good with light winds and partly sunny skies. However on approaching Sondy, an unusual wind reversal brought low cloud, drizzle and fog up the fjord, making a landing below minimums our only option with our available fuel.

Compounding our problem was that Sondy's "always reliable" WW2 military GCA radar "happened to be out" in rain and their "always reliable" SF radio beacon (382 kcs) four miles from the airport also just "happened to be off the air" for its scheduled annual maintenance. Making a back beacon approach from the secondary radio beacon 14 miles down the fjord was our only hope! And wouldn't you know it, PCI had no radar! Our alternate was, at this point, a wheels-up crash-landing on the icecap.

While our minimum altitude for this type of approach was 2,000 feet after crossing the distant radio beacon, we descended to 800 feet, putting us between the hills on either side. Phil, our great navigator, called out our drift readings whenever he caught an occasional glimpse of the ground, but we missed seeing the field on our first approach and pulled up, climbed to 3,000 feet and returned to the beacon. On our second approach, we descended to just 400 feet after passing the beacon, catching intermittent glimpses of the valley below through the rain and fog as Phil called out our drift.

Spotting the field as we passed over, and with precious little fuel left, we reversed course with a steep turn for a hair-raising landing into the wind. While our pulses slowed, the 88 passengers, seemingly unconcerned by our violent antics, poured out of the aircraft in the rain to purchase their souvenirs. After our one-hour refuelling stop, we took off "down fjord," climbed to 3,000 feet towards the beacon, then turned on course toward Oslo. We finally broke out above the cloud and the sun smiled on us once again!

In August that same year, we were returning from Amsterdam and on approaching Keflavik, our initial refuelling stop, one engine revealed a problem and we shut it down. When the engine was inspected on the ground, more than minor damage was discovered and the decision was made to replace the engine! Fortunately Scandinavian Airlines (SAS) had one to spare and my First Officer was tasked with helping the mechanics replace the engine while I took passengers and stewardesses for a bus tour around southern Iceland.

Although the engine change went well, a great many of the electrical connections were not compatible and could not be joined. As a result, even though many engine instruments were quite "dead," we received permission to operate in this fashion, loaded all aboard and flew to Sondrestrom for fuel and a quick engine inspection, then on to Edmonton where the engine was changed again and the borrowed one was returned to Keflavik.

For the federal election held on November 8th 1965, and at Max's invitation, I spent a week flying an Aero Commander 560 (CF-SEX) distributing ballot boxes to the Dew Line stations across the Arctic, receiving $5 per hour "bonus pay." SEX had been used as a VIP commuter aircraft in the Caribbean and we had its bar and all its many extra passenger comforts removed. SEX also came with its normal summer weight oil, and so both engines required 4 hours of preheat with Herman Nelson heaters whenever overnighting in the Arctic. One of the engine's carburetor heat controls was also wired in backwards but we soon learned to accept its many idiosyncrasies.

After a quick checkout on October 18th, I flew to Fort Smith and brought one of the federal candidates and his party back to Edmonton where I renewed my instrument rating. The following day, I flew Max Ward and his candidate to Yellowknife and the day after that, we visited Fort Resolution and back again to Yellowknife. On the 22nd, I took Walter Pokiak, Wardair's dedicated Eskimo engineer east to Baker Lake, the self-described "geographic centre of Canada" where a Mountie's wife who served as the DRO (District Returning Officer) came aboard. These two worked as a team to unload our ballot boxes at airports along the Dew Line or via small parachutes at the several stations we called at when no airport was available.

Next day, after heating the engines at Baker Lake, we "serviced" such places as Eskimo Point, Whale Cove, Rankin Inlet, Chesterfield Inlet, then overnighted at Coral Harbour. Next day, after again heating the engines, we flew to Repulse Bay, Spence Bay, Pelly Bay, Gjoa Haven and Cambridge Bay. Arriving at Cambridge Bay, we advised the ground personnel that we were on a "Federal Contract," at which they graciously ushered us into their warm hangar for the night. In the morning, they asked us for our contract number, then booted us out when we told them we were on contract for our Federal Government, not their Federal Electric Company! But Walter had had a good sleep and our aircraft was toasty warm.

The K Band radar on SEX was truly excellent and we were able to return to Baker Lake flying in solid overcast cloud while "reading" the passing terrain on radar. Following my return to Edmonton and at Max's invitation, I flew Joy around the city one evening to view the sights. On final approach to the airport, our nose gear didn't indicate "green." The

I wish I had taken a photo of CF-SEX with CF-FUN together in the Edmonton hangar!

light tested OK so we flew past the tower and with a powerful light, they checked that our nose gear was indeed down. It turned out to be a defective switch and our landing was thankfully quite uneventful.

Leaving Frobisher Bay for Vancouver one bitterly cold October day on PCI, we shut an engine down when it indicated a problem and dumped much of our fuel to get down to our maximum landing weight. Fifty minutes later, we landed back in Frobisher where damage was discovered in one of the rear cylinders, calling for its replacement. We felt so sorry for Joe, our valiant maintenance engineer, as he battled biting winds for several hours while working at his task behind a sheet of plywood. We took turns handing him parts and tools and our passengers were put up in the games room where some were able to sleep on the pool tables. When we received a message from Edmonton asking why the cylinder change was taking more than seven hours when it was normally only a four-hour job, the answer from Joe was simply not fit to print! I flew a total of 1,064.5 hours in the first 10 months of 1965, *153.5* hours in October alone.

In February 1966, we operated PCI for a fortnight as a "scheduled carrier" for Pacific Western Airlines, operating their Calgary-Edmonton flights while their DC-6 underwent a large maintenance check. The fixed schedule allowed me, as a senior pilot, to take weekends off. I packed our children into the BelAir, tied the toboggan on top and took them all to "our" hill overlooking the Saskatchewan River. Of course the dog insisted on going too and couldn't see why she couldn't ride down on the family toboggan with them. It was quite the sight to see what looked like a dog steering!

While the month of scheduled flying was an interesting month, I was happy to return to the variety our charter operations offered. You might say that I had become "charter oriented"!

We were flying the Edmonton Petroleum Club to Honolulu via Oakland one day and when nearing Honolulu, I shut an engine down when gauges indicated possible damage. After we had feathered the propeller and tidied every thing up, I joked with our passengers that we were simply practicing for the arrival of our three-engine Boeing 727 later that year. However two weeks later, our same crew was returning the Petroleum Club to Edmonton and we had just reached our cruising altitude out of Portland when we again had to shut down the same engine and divert our flight into Vancouver for repairs. Our passengers were not amused as they ended their holidays much later than expected, finally arriving in Edmonton on a hastily-chartered DC-9.

April was a "good month" for I flew *150* hours with the same co-pilot (and no engine problems!), flying charters from Edmonton, Calgary and Grand Prairie to European destinations such as Dusseldorf, Amsterdam, Gatwick, and Copenhagen and then returning our happy passengers after two or three weeks overseas. And so I ended my DC-6 flying on a happy note as I passed the 10,000-hour mark, 6,000 of which were on the good old Douglas DC-6.

WARDAIR 727

Max must have been able to persuade Boeing to sell him one of their aircraft on very favourable terms for until then, no airline was flying Boeings in Canada. And so, in May 1966, we flew from Edmonton down to Seattle to train on one of Boeing's brand new three-engine Boeing 727s. As an introduction to our first experience with jet aircraft, our ground school instructor told us that we would now be leaving the ancient "suck, squeeze, bang and blow" technology and entering the reliable jet-age realm of flight. How right he was! At this point, we were quite used to flying around on three engines and as our new aircraft only had three, we felt quite confident in our abilities to handle that number.

Our flight crews underwent a comprehensive ground school which included learning about "walking beams" and our new Chief Pilot, a senior pilot holding Canadian Airline Transport licence #62 and who had been flying Douglas DC-8s with Air Canada and was therefore "turbine experienced," took the course with us.

When we were introduced to our brand new Boeing 727 (CF-FUN), we nicknamed it "Smokey the Bear" because of the long trail of black smoke coming from its three 12,000-pound-thrust engines (12,000 horse power at 375 mph). Our auxiliary power unit was located back in the tail between the engines so the cockpit was blessedly quiet except for wind noise at higher speeds. I had adopted the practice of using a single ear

Wardair's first passenger jet, the Boeing 727, was a great deal of FUN to fly, while passengers truly enjoyed its quiet speed.

plug for radio communication which I regretted much later, for it offered no protection at all against "wind whistle."

We took extensive flight training of 30 hours each on FUN, enjoying the sense of power as the three engines "spooled up" for take-off. On my final check ride at the Great Falls Montana airport, I extended my landing flare to clear an arrester wire I saw on approaching the runway (which, as it turned out, was retracted) and compressed the tail skid which nearly failed my final ride.

In addition to the two pilots, we carried a navigator and a flight engineer. This engineer was not only acquainted with walking beams and other bits and pieces of the aircraft but operated the flight engineer's station in the cockpit which showed the condition of our three engines as well as the status of all the aircraft's operating systems. He also supervised the refuelling at our underwing refuelling station. We carried the same three stewardesses for our 110 passengers.

FUN was equipped with a self-contained passenger stairway which deployed from below the front entry door, as well as one which lowered from the tail between the engines. This meant that we no longer had to wait while passenger stairs were wheeled into position after our arrival.

Because our jet aircraft required a longer runway for take-off, our operations were transferred to the newly-opened airport at Nisku – about 16 miles south of Edmonton. We truly enjoyed our flights to Europe which halved our DC-6 flying times but required the same fuel stops (30 minutes instead of an hour). Many observers thought we must be operating several 727s, as we were so often seen flying back and forth over northern Canada.

It was quite a revelation to abandon the era of the piston engine and its sometimes cranky *suck, squeeze, bang and blow* technology with the pistons, rings, valves, crankshafts and many other moving parts and enter the world of the reliable revolving jet engine technology where, up to a point, the faster one went, the more horsepower the engines developed. While we enjoyed its modern radar, by flying more than twice as high, we missed seeing the view in the DC-6 of the slowly unfolding terrain two miles below (much closer over the spectacular Greenland fjords and ice cap along the Arctic Circle) as well as the majestic icebergs floating between Greenland and Iceland.

We were taking Max with us to London one day and after our landing at Sondy, Max handed me the keys to his Cadillac and asked that I pick it up from the airport terminal and drive it to its normal parking spot below the MacDonald Hotel. On my return, I found it parked in a no-parking zone, right in front of the Edmonton terminal where it was carefully looked after by the guards on duty! And no parking ticket.

On June 2nd, after twenty landings in regular passenger service under supervision, I was once again flying as pilot in command. There were no restrictions on speed below 10,000 feet at the time and we enjoyed departing Edmonton and accelerating to 340 knots (390 mph) before commencing a normal climb. There was also no requirement to use landing lights at lower altitudes, and at twilight we probably looked like a shadow thundering upward, leaving a trail of smoke.

The interior of the aircraft was quiet and very comfortable in cruise and I enjoyed pointing out to our passengers the dark near-vertical line rising from the after part of the wing marking the boundary between subsonic and supersonic airflow, known as the "shock wave" as we cruised along at 84% of the speed of sound!

Flight planning for jet aircraft required that we carry not only fuel to our destination but also fuel to a suitable alternate and 30 minutes reserve (piston engine operations require 45). Occasionally we found ourselves a bit tight for fuel for our intended flight. This occurred mostly on flights from Sondy to western Canada and so a method was developed to increase the fuel capacity of our aircraft. This involved jacking up the main wheels on one side of the aircraft, then filling that wing's overflow tip tank. The other wing's tip tank was likewise filled and we would then depart, sometimes leaving behind a trail of fuel from our wingtips! In this way, we were able to fly trips such as Sondy to Vancouver or Keflavik to Edmonton (or return) in flights that lasted just over 6 hours.

Following our landing in Sondy one day, we were waiting with engines idling just south of the active runway for an SAS aircraft to depart when our flight engineer noticed that passengers were wandering about on the taxiway below us! A quick glance at his panel confirmed that our rear door was not closed and an inquiry revealed that our stewardess at the back believed we had parked at the terminal and so had deplaned our passengers via the rear air stairs between the idling engines. Our auxiliary power unit in the tail was almost as noisy as the engines and it was difficult to determine if the engines were indeed running. However we had given no permission to deplane our passengers and our apologetic stewardesses quickly rounded them up and re-boarded them for the short taxi to the terminal on the north side of the runway.

We landed at Helsinki, Finland in June and dropped off our passengers. On our departure, we had been cleared for take-off but as we were entering the active runway, the tower urgently asked us to vacate it a.s.a.p as an aircraft on short final had declared an emergency. We were able to oblige using our reverse thrust and *backed off* the active runway!

As our three engines were high-up in the tail, they didn't blow up a lot of ground debris.

During pilot training for our semi-annual IFR (instrument flying rating) checks, our cleaners worked on board, grooming the aircraft for the afternoon flight. They worked hard and quickly, for the aircraft didn't make money on the ground and its time on the ground was therefore quite limited. During this training period, the cleaners had work to do and the pilots needed precious air time for training. So a flight training crew would board the aircraft and, following their pre-flight checks, would start up, take off and proceed to practice steep turns and other manoeuvres while the aircraft was being cleaned and vacuumed.

One of these manoeuvres required a simulated pressurization failure which necessitated an emergency descent and so, nearing 35,000 feet, word was sent back to "buckle up." "Depressurization" was then called, oxygen masks were donned, throttles were closed, speed brakes were raised, and a steep turn was initiated as FUN adopted a steep nose down attitude. The crew in training then dove at maximum dive speed down to 10,000 feet when oxygen masks could be removed. This, while our nimble cleaners enjoyed their "work break" in the nearest available seat! When flying "normally" once more, they resumed their cleaning chores while the crew practiced their approaches and missed approaches. Following its final landing, the aircraft was fuelled, catering was boarded, passengers were loaded and the aircraft departed on time, now with its operating crew, generally for Sondy.

Captains were issued credit cards to buy jet fuel for our hungry engines and soon discovered that while the cheapest fuel was to be had in Amsterdam at just 8 cents per Imperial Gallon, Sondrestrom ran a close second at 9 cents. The company really didn't mind that fuel stop which often occurred twice a day. Our passengers didn't seem to mind either, with cigarettes at a dollar a carton and spirits at a dollar a bottle.

Wardair tried someone's bright idea of positioning a crew in Sondy to operate flights from there to London and back. However, after by-passing Sondy once or twice due to weather which required either the outbound crew to fly to London and back to Sondy, or the Sondy crew to fly to London and all the way home to Edmonton, it was cancelled. And the flight crews hated those triple bunks provided in Sondy!

Sometimes after arriving in Prestwick (which always greeted us with bagpipes playing gaily), our schedule required that the inbound crew leave from London several days later. The outbound crew had driven Wardair's 7-seat VW minibus up from London and we used it to return our crew to London. An added bonus, of course, was the sightseeing, and crews organized their own meals as well as bed-and-breakfast accommodation while en route.

One day, our minibus lunch stop happened to take place on the very edge of the grounds of Windsor Castle. We had just sat down and opened our picnic lunches when we noticed a typical English "bobby" riding down the long road from the castle.

"Did you not know that you are trespassing on *Her Majesty's Long Walk?*" he said with a very red face. *"Go!"*

And so we packed up and left, although we had fully intended to stop off after lunch to pay our respects....

FUN was leased to a South American company that first winter and with full pay, I seized the opportunity to take one full semester of university training. Returning to fly again in May 1967, we flew from all over western Canada to all sorts of European destinations and I think our flight planner/navigators simply drew a six-hour circle around Sondy and considered that anything within the circle was fair game as a destination and passed the information to the sales staff. In addition to Edmonton and Calgary, we flew passengers from Regina, Saskatoon, Victoria, Vancouver and Winnipeg, not only to our usual destinations of Gatwick and Prestwick, but also to Shannon, Amsterdam, Copenhagen, Helsinki, Oslo, Dusseldorf, Belfast, Glasgow and Stockholm's Arlanda Airport. [I just wanted to emphasize that charter flying can be anything but routine and dull.]

In September, we proved that our 727 could operate quite well on just two engines when we ferried our aircraft from Calgary to Edmonton with one engine inoperative. It was just a great aircraft and I never had a problem with it. Flying was especially satisfying several times that fall when, following the long hop from Calgary to Sondy and on our final approach into London, the welcome view of Gatwick's approach lights appeared out of the mist just as we reached our minimum approach altitude!

During the winter of 1967/68 we operated trips to New Orleans, Grand Cayman Island, Nassau, Kingston and Montego Bay. I took advantage of our Caribbean stop one fine day to go for a swim off our parking spot near the end of the Montego Bay's runway while waiting for our passengers and fuel.

In February, we began our flights to Honolulu with an interesting route which took us via Anchorage Alaska due to the odd jet stream. After a week of beach time, we flew back to Toronto the long way round via Oakland and Montreal. Ten days later, we returned to Toronto and then operated the flight to Kingston, Montego Bay, Nassau and back to Toronto. The following day saw us operate through Oakland to Honolulu and then home!

Some time after I had retired, pilots were surveyed to find out why those on Caribbean and South Pacific routes developed skin cancer more often than those on the polar routes. One theory had been that this was due to the higher tropopause at lower latitudes which allowed more ultraviolet radiation on the pilots. A quick check however pointed to the lengthy beach time "suffered" by the flight crews on those Caribbean and Pacific routes. I am still today annually receiving the "nitrogen treatment" for pre-cancerous appearances on my head.

Winds in the upper atmosphere were rather difficult to forecast and often times our navigators reported winds that were at wide variance to those the met office projected. The jet stream in the mid-latitudes in winter changed direction sometimes quite violently and rough air could be very difficult to predict. We radioed our position reports and flight conditions every 5 or 10 degrees of longitude and the met forecasters used these and other reports to update their charts for subsequent flights.

In March 1968, I was studying for my final exams at U of A. After completing one trip to Honolulu via Oakland and return, I packed up my study books and left for Toronto, Oakland and then a week of beach/study time in Honolulu. Unfortunately, however, my bags with all my studies went somewhere else and I was left "stranded on the beach" with no books to study! I flew home at the end of March, caught up with my bags and books and wrote my exams anyway – and probably just scraped through.

While we had thought that our family of four children was complete, it is evident that God had other plans and Joy kept getting messages that we should adopt another girl. In fact, Joy actually *knew* when the baby had been born! We called the agency which happened to have our file still on hand and Jennifer arrived that spring in good time to take her with us to the cabin. We never regretted accepting God's choice and Jennifer is always thanking Joy for listening to God!

In May, we returned to our London operation and on our return, we flew from Sondy to our present home town of Victoria in just 6 hours. As well as Gatwick that summer, we also operated to Oslo, Copenhagen, Dusseldorf and Stockholm.

After finishing our 727 service in October, three of us were asked to ferry PCI, our great old DC-6 with its unused Dutch emergency equipment, from Edmonton's municipal airport to its International Airport where it was to be stored. As we were checking our flight controls before take-off, we noticed that they seemed to be very stiff until we ran the before take-off check and realized with a laugh that we had forgotten to remove our flight control's mechanical gust lock which the 727 didn't need. We left our wheels down for the flight and Don did a great job of placing them gently onto the runway for our arrival.

My logbook shows more than 1,500 hours flying the 727.

It was certainly a good thing that our winter flying was not as hectic as our summers, for I was able to continue taking a couple of courses at the university each winter. I will always be grateful to the students (usually the girls) who allowed me to have a copy of their notes for the price of a piece of carbon paper when I was away on a trip.

WARDAIR 707

In March of 1969, as our crews were then "turbine experienced," we had a shortened ground school course at the Boeing plant before "flying" Boeing's very realistic 707 flight simulator for 20 hours and the "real thing" for a further 18. Their simulator was deemed to be acceptable for our semi-annual aircraft and instrument proficiency checks so we no longer had to accomplish these in the aircraft while our cleaners readied the aircraft for our next passengers. We found the aircraft to be surprisingly easy to handle with an outboard engine at idle, and were even able to successfully manage handling two engines "out" on one side.

CF-FAN was one of our two brand new Boeing 707 "combis" (passenger/freighters) while our second carried the registration CF-ZYP. In passenger configuration, each carried 180 passengers (requiring five in the cabin) and each of their four engines developed 18,000 pounds of reliable and smoke-free thrust. However we did miss our self-contained passenger stairs and had to rely once again on ground staff to trundle stairs up to us on each arrival.

With the arrival of our two 707s in addition to our 727, our sales staff had to be effectively tripled and sales offices were opened across Canada. More ground personnel and flight crews were also hired and trained and many new faces appeared on our flight line. Our hard working and well-liked stewardesses were also due for a "face lift" and, as male personnel were added and objected to the term "stewards," those who worked in our cabins became known as "cabin attendants."

Airlines were often called unflattering names by the various flight crews. Trans-Canada Air Lines was known as "Trash Can Airline" until, after landing one of its DC-8s in a cabbage patch short of the runway at Heathrow Airport, it became known as "Trans-Cabbage Airlines" and after it took the name of Air Canada, it was called "Air Chance." United Airlines became known as "Untied Airlines," Canadian Pacific Airlines was "Crash and Panic," Trans World Airlines was "Tiggly Wiggly," PWA was "Please Wait Awhile" and Wardair was referred to as "Weird-air."

Flying across the Atlantic non-stop was a real treat in some respects, although we missed the refuelling stops where we could stretch our legs while passengers purchased their souvenirs. I'm sure that the Sondy fuelers and souvenir shop missed us even more! As summer came, my first 707 flight took us from Vancouver to Gatwick (non-stop!) and returning via Frankfurt. Two days later, I carried Mom Tooley with Joy and our son Ian to Gatwick, then returned via Windsor and Toronto. The 707 certainly had "long legs" and from western Canada we ranged all over Europe with them – Athens, Rome, Amsterdam, Frankfurt, Prestwick, etc.

As a side-note, we took Mom Tooley to the UK several times and each time, to show her gratitude to Wardair, she sent Max a special English tea cup and saucer. I'm sure that he received very few such gifts of gratitude!

On August 1st, after leaving Edmonton in ZYP with a full passenger load, we discovered that we were unable to pressurize our aircraft for some reason and had to return. However we far exceeded our maximum landing weight and had to "dump" thousands of gallons of fuel which we spread all over the farming area north of Edmonton. One of our pilots had his home in this area and swore that he could still smell kerosene for days.

After the balky valve had been replaced, a test flight was called for. However after completing another weight and balance calculation, we discovered that we were far outside our allowable flying range with baggage in the aft hold and no passengers aboard, and so would be too tail heavy for flight. After unloading most of the baggage and conducting a short test flight, we loaded all on board and had an uneventful flight to Dusseldorf followed by an empty flight to Gatwick where another crew took over.

Next day, we took ZYP to Goteborg, Sweden where we picked up our passengers and flew them to Montreal. Three days later, we took passengers on FAN from Toronto to Ellinikon International in Athens (which was decommissioned in 2001), then flew back to Gatwick. Two days later, we flew ZYP to Calgary. [I think one can detect just a hint of our hectic 1969 operation!]

While our Bel Air proved to be a great car for Joy to use at the lake, we discovered its limitations during our family's trip to the Rockies. Its little 6-cylinder 100-hp engine could not overcome the handicap of its two-speed transmission and we called it "the Rolls Can Hardly" because, as Brian said, it rolls downhill and can hardly climb back up again. Therefore, after our family's stay at the cottage in 1969, we traded it in for a hefty 1967 Dodge Monaco station wagon.

We made brief visits to sun spots such as Honolulu and Puerto Vallarta that winter and on one trip to Honolulu, I experienced a "close encounter." I had developed a habit of maintaining a high cruise altitude until close to our destination, as the air was usually smoother and time and fuel were saved. Approaching Honolulu, Air Traffic Control cleared us to descend to 10,000 feet. This was prior to long-range ground-based radar and we advised ATC when we left our cruising altitude of 39,000 feet. We proceeded to make a rapid descent through cloud only to pop out at 10,000 feet, right beside a Northwest Orient DC-8 which had chosen a more leisurely (and therefore much slower) descent!

The 707 was a very reliable aircraft and we enjoyed flying the latest model which came equipped with 2 "air bottles," either of which could start an outboard engine using its stored compressed air. Compressed air from any operating engine could then be used to start the other engines. On one occasion, upon arrival in Warsaw with passengers, we shut down our engines and waited patiently while police checked our passenger and crew manifests. Our passengers then deplaned, using a rather antiquated ladder while our returning passengers waited patiently behind high barbed wire fencing. Other than the fuel truck, the ladder was the only ground equipment we saw on the tarmac.

We refuelled as the passengers waited quietly – with none of the happy chatter we had become used to – and seemed very relieved and happy to climb aboard. A PWA 707 was stuck there, waiting for a compressed air cart to come from another airport to enable them to start their engines. However, as soon as our passengers were seated and their baggage stowed, we used one of our two fixed air bottles to start #4 engine and were away in no time to the relief of our passengers who were most happy to escape from their visit behind the Iron Curtain.

In 1970, we concentrated once again on Europe and on May 6th flying ZYP out of London, we were experiencing very strong beam winds at 31,000 feet. Approaching Pole Hill (Manchester), Air Traffic Control called, asking us to turn right 15 degrees as they had traffic climbing through our altitude, then a further 15 and yet another. We suddenly saw a speck ahead and just to our right, instantly disengaged the autopilot and rolled sharply left to avoid it. We reported our "near miss" after a charter DC-9 carrying soccer supporters hurtled past at over 1,000 miles per hour closing speed (I kept the transcript). It was startling to observe how quickly the oncoming aircraft grew bigger! It was also startling to be told later that Joy, awakened from a sound sleep by the single word "PRAY", had knelt beside the bed and, once assurance was received, had climbed back in and fallen fast asleep! Sure enough, when we later compared notes and accounting for the eight hours time difference, it was the same time as I had been over Manchester!

On June 5th, after leaving Toronto, ATC called to notify us of a reported bomb on board. We again dumped thousands of gallons of our fuel, this time all over Lake Ontario, and returned to land at Toronto. Nothing was found however and, after refuelling, we again left for Gatwick.

In July we flew FAN to Belfast and then my log book shows us picking up passengers at LYZA (?) which is no longer in use, taking them to Toronto, then back to Dublin for another load going to Toronto.

On one of my trips to Amsterdam, I purchased two child seats for bicycles which were at the time unknown in Edmonton. I had flown our bicycles home from Gatwick and the boys each had their own, so with five bicycles and two carriers, we were able to take our whole family for Sunday outings. Helmets were as yet unheard of and with Patty running along beside us, our family took up the whole street!

I never flew the 707 in freighter configuration although many of our Toronto crews did, bringing loads of tomatoes up from the Azores among other things. In October 1970, we were operating passenger charters to Faro in Portugal, and Max was dreaming of opening a cruise resort at Lanzarote, Azores and carrying tomatoes back to Toronto when empty, but passenger seat stowage remained a problem. Later that month, I became a passenger, "deadheading" in our 727 (FUN) from Edmonton to Vancouver. Then, after boarding our passengers, the operating crew chose the northern route from Edmonton to Brussels with a fuel stop at our old stop of Sondy. I enjoyed my short reacquaintance but no, I didn't buy any souvenirs.

Early in 1971 we were flying passengers from the Prairies (Saskatoon, Regina, Calgary and Edmonton) to sunspots such as Honolulu and Puerto Vallarta. We became used to seeing them return after a week or two to their icy-cold departure points in shorts and flip-flops, quickly melting their wonderful tans as they descended the stairs and dashed across the ramp to the terminal building. It is very difficult to picture and plan for one's return to a frigid sub-zero airport apron after one has spent two weeks in the tropics.

In February, I made another flight to Hong Kong's Kai Tak airport and on our approach was amazed by the rapid growth of the tall apartment buildings on our approach path over the checkerboard to runway 13. And once again, I returned via Tokyo's Haneda airport.

On March 24th, 1971 while in Honolulu for a few days, I received a checkout on a Piper Cherokee 6, a seven-passenger aircraft and received an American private pilot licence which enabled me to fly our seven-person flight crew from Honolulu to Maui for the day whenever our Honolulu stops permitted. On one occasion, we were returning from Maui above a low overcast cloud and I received permission to track in on their localizer. Lacking a glide slope on approaching Honolulu, the friendly tower operator used his radar and gave me a "step-down approach" which worked out very well. We broke out of cloud at 1,500 feet with the Honolulu runway dead ahead.

In April, we were flying FAN from Edmonton to Honolulu at 35,000 feet and as we neared our west coast, suddenly noticed a crack in one of our front windows which required an immediate descent! Upon receiving permission, we quickly descended to 12,000 feet and as we were below our maximum landing weight we landed at Vancouver for a quick inspection. As no replacement was available for such a rare occurrence, we unloaded passengers and their baggage and flew to Seattle where a new window was quickly installed by Boeing, then returned to Vancouver where our Honolulu-bound passengers were patiently waiting and off we went to Honolulu.

Wanting to travel with our family and "see a bit of the country," our family rented a little Boler holiday trailer in Camrose and towed it south to Canmore in southern Alberta. After stocking it with supplies, we explored the beautiful forestry trunk road north. Ian and Brian slept in the wagon, David and Brenda slept on the settee and Joy and I slept on the dinette table that made into a bed. And Jennifer? Why, she slept soundly on the floor with Patty! It was a delightful holiday – even if the propane fridge didn't work.

I have been asked if I had flown to very many of the Caribbean islands. While this area was normally handled by our Toronto-based crews, the Edmonton crews sometimes flew trips for them and April saw us flying south to Aruba, an island 20 miles off the coast of Venezuela, and returning passengers to Windsor. Among the more interesting places that year, we flew to Vienna in August, to Athens in September to Malaga,

Spain and also Nice, France in October before returning to our Hawaiian schedule the following month.

In January 1972, with the Canadian Air Traffic Control once more on strike, we flew ZYP one night at a low altitude to keep us below controlled airspace from Edmonton to Great Falls, Montana. Turning west, we landed in Seattle, boarded our Vancouver passengers and took off for Honolulu. The following day we flew our Vancouver-bound passengers in FAN to Seattle, then we ferried the aircraft to Great Falls where we descended and flew VFR (Visual Flight Rules) to Edmonton, again a night flight and not much sightseeing, although I'm sure that we startled some sleeping people as we roared by overhead so late at night.

In February, we were scheduled to fly FAN from Calgary to Zurich, Switzerland. As we had been warned of extensive ATC delays there, we carried several hours of extra fuel which was a good thing, for even with good tail winds we held overhead Zurich in lazy circles for three hours before being permitted to land and our flight took a total of 12 hours. Two weeks later, we returned to Zurich, collected our passengers and flew them back to Calgary against stiff head winds, taking just 10 hours.

The jet aircraft proved to be much more trouble free than the piston-powered aircraft and charter flying continued to be interesting as it was so varied. In one four-day trip in April, I flew from Calgary to Germany, then to Gatwick, Toronto, Windsor, Aruba, Windsor and back to Toronto. Then in July, I flew from Vancouver to Prestwick, to Gatwick, Malaga, Toronto, Freeport, Toronto, Gatwick and back to Edmonton in four days. In December, after flying from Edmonton, we held for two hours overhead Manchester while waiting for the fog to lift enough to permit us to land. Even our semi-annual instrument flying checks, now carried out by our chief pilot in the simulator, were seldom just routine. My university studies had been completed earlier that spring and I had received my basic degree.

As I had been scheduled to fly from Vancouver in early September, we drove our whole family to Vancouver in late August in order to celebrate both Brenda's and my mother's birthdays. While the two adults in the front seat were buckled in, we converted the back of our Dodge wagon into a large cargo compartment in which children (and Patty) were free to roam around and read or play with their toys. Except for my uniform and briefcase, our suitcases were all on the roof rack under a tarpaulin securely tied to the rails.

Nearing our destination, we were driving down a long hill in the Fraser Canyon when we were startled by the shadow of our tarpaulin flapping above us. We could do nothing about it because of the traffic and sure enough, at the bottom of the hill it suddenly "let go" and suitcases started leaving our vehicle! Shortly after, I managed to pull off the road, ran back and gathered up the scattered bits and pieces which had been clobbered several times by the traffic, threw everything into the back with our children and we drove on.

On arrival at the Sylvia Hotel, we carried the remains to our rooms, where we found that very little real damage had occurred, although a heavy truck had left its studded tire marks on some of Joy's clothing including her underwear, enabling her to boast to her friends that she now had the only "studded bra" in existence!

Looking back over our first four years of Boeing flying, we didn't fly the long monthly or yearly hours we had done in our propeller-driven aircraft. But then neither did we "enjoy" the long layovers at our destinations. My logbook shows 2,400 hours flying the 707.

As Joy was not at daily work outside the home, she was available to both ours and our neighbour's children and became known as a "mother confessor" to many as she fed them fresh bread from the oven and bandaged their cuts. Our house became a place where working moms could rely on for their children to be when they came home. I particularly remember two little boys who were sent to their grandma's house several blocks away wearing shoes without sox in freezing weather. One had wet himself when Joy found them and thawed them out. They then spent many happy days playing with Jennifer.

WARDAIR 747

In 1969, the Boeing 747 began flying passengers for Pan American World Airways and two years later, with Trans-Canada Airlines which had become Air Canada in 1965. With four big thirsty engines, it proved to be economical only with a full passenger load and so Max thought it to be quite suited for charter flying as we generally operated with full loads. Thus in April 1973, we returned to Boeing's plant in Seattle for our third ground school course on turbines and then 23 hours in their full-motion flight simulator trainer under the direction of a Boeing check pilot. Unlike our old DC-6 simulators, these could realistically complete all the manoeuvres necessary for certifying pilots and flight engineers as competent to fly the 747, although initially costing almost as much as the real airplane!

We also watched a movie of the 747 certification process. In it, a maximum load of Boeing passenger-actors demonstrated that they could evacuate their 747 aircraft, via a randomly-chosen half of its eleven evacuation chutes, within 90 seconds at night! "Leaping Lizards" is the expression that came to my mind.

Additionally, we were trained on the recently developed INS (Inertial Navigation System) which would replace our friendly navigators. The aircraft flew the course dictated by the middle course as calculated by three Collins INS platforms and whenever their tracks crossed, the aircraft turned and followed the "new" middle course, which was a mite bit disconcerting at first. While Max thought we needed just two INS platforms on each flight, keeping one for spare, we finally convinced him of the very real necessity of three.

The aircraft could be quite intimidating on a walk around, with its 16 main wheels and two under the nose. We were told that each tire would be checked and recapped after 100 landings. I have been asked if we ever had a flat tire and after 17 years on the 747, I only recall having one, after my flight from Paris to Quebec City in July 1987.

Aircraft training took place at Moses Lake where the runways were deceptive as they were double the normal width, but it was amazing how quickly we adjusted to our cockpit's three-storey altitude and we had just 6.5 hours flying the real aircraft to prove it before taking our final instrument check ride.

Our small Vancouver base required just two 747 crews and during the summer, the other senior captain and myself moved our families to Victoria. Joy was puzzled as to why I chose Victoria over a Vancouver suburb, for it would involve extensive commuting. I simply thought that it would be a better place in which to raise our family. [As an added incentive, Victoria only has half the rainfall of Vancouver.]

We were able to sell our "designer home" in Edmonton for $53,000 and bought a relatively new home on the Gordon Head oceanfront for $69,500. I drove the Dodge wagon to Victoria with Joy and four of our children while Ian, our eldest son, drove the Volvo to Victoria after finishing his summer job of counselling at the Sylvan Lake church camp.

Our new home was ideally suited for our family of seven, for it had a large (30 x 18) living room, an adequate dining room, and a kitchen and family eating area which led out onto the sundeck. There were five bedrooms and three bathrooms and the only change we made in almost 40 years was the addition of a sunporch. One December there were 100 young people in our home at a gathering close to Christmas!

I commuted to and from Vancouver for 17 years using PWA Convairs, Time Air Short 360s and Air Canada Dash 8s when available. Mostly however, I used BC Ferries and bought a reconditioned 1972 orange-coloured VW Beetle from a fellow Wardair pilot for that purpose, paying $2,000 for it. Following a ferry crossing to Vancouver, I trotted over to where I had parked the VW on the causeway (which was free), and either drove to the Vancouver airport or took advantage of either my brother Ian's or my mother's hospitality when remaining overnight in Vancouver.

The VW was trouble free but came equipped with a heater which used more fuel than the engine. Each year, I brought it to Victoria for servicing and our daughter Brenda enjoyed driving it for a week or two. Our first grandson called it "Auntie Brenda's racing car"! I had no idea it was being attacked by the salt spray until a few years later at the Vancouver airport when trying to jack it up to fix a flat tire and while the jack came up, the car didn't! After causeway parking became unavailable, we traded it in on a new Hyundai which remained in Victoria and received a $2,000 trade-in allowance for the Beetle.

Our Gordon Head home was close to a lovely little park and the playground became quite well used by our children including Patty, who waited patiently for her turn on the slide with the children calling out, "It's Patty's turn!" and helping her up the ladder. She slid down, ears flying behind, then queued up to climb the ladder and slide down again.

Wardair took delivery of its first 747 aircraft, otherwise known as "Boeing's Queen of the Skies", in May 1973. Its registration of CF-DJC was the registration of Max Ward's original little three-passenger de-Havilland Fox Moth and we dubbed it "De Jumbo Charter" for it came equipped with 440 seats on the main floor and 16 on the upper deck behind the flight crew. The aircraft wasn't brand new, but an original which had been returned to Boeing after very little usage.

Each cockpit crew consisted of two pilots and a flight engineer, while our navigators remained on the ground planning our flights, accomplished "flight following" and organizing our fuel pick-ups. If memory serves me, each aircraft came equipped with 14 lavatories.

While only 12 flight attendants were required, Max insisted that up to 18 including a supervisor be carried to maintain his first class standards!

There were no extra fees such as baggage and seat selection while "first class" three-course hot meals served on Royal Doulton china complete with monogrammed "silverware" and a large selection of beverages were all complimentary!

The 747 was a lumbering aircraft which could be counted on to burn an impressive average of 3,000 Imperial gallons (12 tons!) of kerosene per hour. The passenger boarding stairs had to reach from the ground to the second floor and baggage containers and tractors were deemed to be most essential to move them around.

One real advantage of our INS system of navigation was that it showed our wind direction and speed minute by minute and it was a real eye opener to see such rapid wind direction and speed changes as we crossed the jet stream. However we did miss the presence of our friendly hard-working navigators.

Max Ward initially thought that a rapid turnaround could be accomplished by off-loading our 456 incoming passengers via the left front door and down the stairway to the ramp while the cleaning crew climbed the rear stairway and cleaned behind them. Then, behind the new crew, our outgoing 456 passengers could climb the back stairway and enter the cabin as the cleaning crew was finishing.

This idea was rapidly forgotten as airports gradually installed expensive jetways to replace stairways as the normal method of accessing the aircraft and preventing passengers from using the tarmac. However not all airports were equipped with jetways, and many destinations required passengers to exit terminals onto the ramp, then either walk to the aircraft or climb into busses which took them to the stairway and they then climbed the two storeys to our passenger cabin.

My first 747 charter flight took place on May 13th 1973 with a Boeing check pilot seated on the hard jump seat behind me. We flew from Vancouver to Gatwick, then to Toronto and back to Gatwick, and the fifth day back to Vancouver. After a few days off, it was back to Gatwick, then Toronto, back to Gatwick and finally to Vancouver, all with a Boeing check pilot observing. Our next flight, also to Gatwick,

Top: *These were the "good old days" before 9/11 after which passenger security became an issue and passenger loading ramps came into being. Passengers never lingered on the ground after it was covered with snow!*

Above: *Max Ward's initial four-seat Fox Moth surrounded by his Boeings. (Photo by George Hunter)*

had a Ministry of Transport check pilot along to observe our operation and thereafter, our three-man flight crew was entirely on its own.

We quickly realized that, while the increase in salary was certainly very nice, the flights had taken on a decidedly scheduled look about them – they were so routine. Varied flights were taken over mainly by our 727 and 707s and later the Douglas DC-10s that Wardair purchased, and much of the flying shifted to the new base in Toronto which became Wardair's main operating base.

Commuting by air from Victoria to Vancouver had its squeaky moments. I used to leave home for the Victoria airport in the red Volvo about 30 minutes before departure, flash my pass at the ticket agent on the way to the ramp and board the waiting aircraft. Sometimes the commuter aircraft was delayed for one reason or another but there was usually another one expected shortly. Sometimes, however, the first aircraft had filled up and the jump seat on the second had also been taken. One day, I had to phone Vancouver that I had been delayed and to please ask the co-pilot and engineer to complete the aircraft checks for me. I finally arrived, climbed into the cockpit, we started the engines and left on schedule, but it was close.

Original engines on CF-DJC were -3s (dash threes) with 43,000 pounds of thrust and were equipped with auxiliary bypass doors. They were very touchy – so touchy in fact that we frequently had to shut a cranky engine down due to a compressor stall, then relight it sometime after we reached our cruise altitude. This was just a bit disconcerting at first, particularly at night when flames were seen coming from the front of the engine! The upgraded -7 (dash seven) engines which were later installed were a great improvement.

One of our flight engineers was a great raconteur and when we reached cruising altitude, would offer up his latest joke. The punch line was always followed by his stomping foot which had never bothered the baggage compartment below us in the 707 but in the 747 was quite disconcerting to the passengers "downstairs" – especially when it unlatched

We thought nothing of cramming two adults, five children and our replacement dog, a Golden Retriever, into our 13-foot-long Boler trailer for meals during inclement weather. We were young then and a pup tent and station wagon helped.

the luggage bins above their heads! Our flight attendants became quite used to explaining this to our front end passengers.

As we still had a couple of years of lease on the cottage at Sylvan Lake, we bought a Boler trailer for our trip to Alberta. After driving the family to Calgary, Joy dropped me off and drove the family to Sylvan while I worked several trips before joining them. We returned in August and in subsequent years, used the trailer for many enjoyable camping trips with our diminishing family as the older ones began working during the summers.

Fall 1973 brought its usual mix of more interesting flying, with flights to Prestwick where the sound of bagpipes still greeted our passengers. The autumn's normal London fog required positioning crews on other carriers so that returning flights would not suffer delays due to mandatory rest times. The smaller charter companies quite enjoyed all this extra business.

One break in my 747 flying routine to Britain was a checkout in the Victoria Flying Club's Cessna 172, followed by a flight with three of our five children. My checkout ride with a young Victoria Flying Club instructor became interesting after he idled the engine and asked me to do a practice forced landing (without power). Since I had been a flying instructor, I was quite prepared for this event, had my landing field already picked out, and side-slipped down to within a few feet of it. As we put on full power to climb away, the sudden noise quite startled a lady over a nearby fence who was hanging out the washing in her back yard! Although commercial flying kept me busy, I still enjoyed flying the Club's Cessnas from time to time.

Our family always bought a Christmas tree to decorate in time for Christmas. 1973 was no exception and I drove our family to the local shopping centre to pick one out. We parked and trooped over to select our tree while Patty minded the car, for she could be a nuisance where trees were concerned. As it was bitterly cold, I left the engine running while we searched through the rows for the perfect tree when there was a sudden crash followed by the sound of falling glass. We saw that our Dodge wagon had driven into a lamp post and the light had shattered! Patty, anxious at being left behind, had put her paws on the steering wheel the better to check on us. Her paws had slipped through onto the gear shift lever, moving it from *park* to *drive* and the car drove forward into the lamp post! She so hated being left out of things.

I made a trip to Honolulu on December 23rd, returning early next morning after a duty day of almost 18 hours. That first winter we often flew DJC from Toronto, Windsor or Montreal to the Caribbean sunspots (mostly Barbados), and our sales people were continually busy selling winter flights from Canada to the Caribbean or Honolulu and summer flights to European destinations.

In March 1974, I operated a flight from Winnipeg to Honolulu and was there for a week. Taking advantage of this time of "suffering," I visited the Dillingham Air Base on the north side of the island where a glider instructor introduced me to his world of silent flight. He checked me out on a Schweitzer I-15 side-by-side glider which was towed aloft to 1,500 feet and the instructor then released the tow line. After "feeling" the controls and quietly enjoying this noiseless flight, I went back the next day and was sent solo for another hour of quiet enjoyment, soaring back and forth with the birds!

It was such a wonderful experience, being quietly held aloft by the NE trades blowing against the ridge of hills on the north side of the island. I could soar around back and forth along the ridge just as long as I wished. I made several trips to that airport over time, flying a total of seven hours towards the ten hours required for a glider licence. That was not to be, however, for Wardair became much more efficient and I then rarely had a day off in Honolulu.

After shutting down a cranky engine on my flight from the Caribbean to Toronto on April 1st, I experienced my first real three-engine landing on the 747 which proved quite uneventful. It was however, as I reminded our passengers, April Fool's Day.

Flights from Barbados to a fireman's strike in Toronto and then a customs work-to-rule slowdown delayed all flights and sent our crews scurrying to operate from either Niagara Falls or Detroit to maintain some semblance of a schedule. It was also a problem to get our passengers and crews to where the aircraft was at the time and bus companies did a roaring business.

Wardair was fined one day following my push-back from our Gatwick gate just two minutes before the hour. This two minutes allowed our push-back tug to unhook and we could start our engines and start taxiing under our own power *on* the hour. This was the time that we always used in our log books and we called this "on time." One irate passenger arrived at the boarding station on the hour and placed a legal complaint with the airport manager. Wardair was then fined for leaving "early"! We all live and learn.

On flights to and from Honolulu, Wardair became widely known for its full-service flights complete with "sunshine breakfasts" and a selection of four-course dinners served on Royal Doulton china and fine Wardair cutlery. A popular selection was the delicious "lobster thermidor" which in reality was New Zealand crayfish! Our passengers much enjoyed the service, although china and silverware were frequently stolen for souvenirs and we later heard that the Wards had not even been able to save a set for themselves.

In wintertime, before the advent of passenger-loading fingers in Saskatoon, we again watched in some amusement while our passengers descended the long stairway from our aircraft, still dressed in their aloha shirts, shorts and thongs and climbed laboriously over the snowdrifts and into the terminal building in minus 30 degree weather.

Another interesting flight from Saskatoon came about after the major airlines refused to carry passengers who were dependent on oxygen breathing equipment. Wardair responded to the challenge and I carried at least 40 of these happy "oxygen-users" on one of my flights from Saskatoon to Honolulu without any problems. Of course, the folk in our greatly enlarged "no smoking section" shared by these happy "oxygen users" were more than happy to abstain from lighting up during this flight.

On August 13th 1974, I rented the club's four-seat Cessna. With Joy beside me, David (13) and Brenda (10) climbed into the back seat and we tucked little Jennifer (7) behind them into the baggage compartment. Fog rolled in as we approached Tofino and after a second landing attempt, we called the airport to say we were returning to Victoria. Suddenly a wail from the very back was heard: "But, Daddy, I've got to pee" which caused us to divert to nearby Alberni, the field where I had instructed from in 1956. After an uneventful pee stop in the warm sunshine, we flew back to Victoria where I got bawled out for landing at an "unlicensed airfield"!

I was flying the Cessna 150 with David one day and elected to practice an approach at the private Central Saanich airport known as "Butler's Field." As I opened the throttle for our "missed approach" a sinking sensation made me acutely aware of a large tree just ahead of us when I noticed that David had his knee under the flap switch and had raised our flaps! Overriding his knee, I put them back down and we just missed brushing that tree.

Some years later, when Brian was taking flight training at Trinity Western College, the two of us were on our way to Campbell River in the Cessna 150 under sunny skies and 70°F temperatures when our engine started to run rough. We landed at the little strip at Ladysmith and when nothing could be found to cause the problem, we sheepishly had to admit that we had been caught with a simple matter of carburetor ice and should have applied the available carburetor heat to clear it. I flew many uneventful flights with the flying club until my family had grown up and were not as interested.

However we enjoyed taking our children to Hawaii or London when I had a layover or was on holidays and they were almost always interested in going! My pilot friend of our near disaster at Sondy was taking a trip to Hawaii one day and I asked him if he would mind taking 14-year-old son David along as I would be arriving the following day for two days and could bring him home with me. David felt very important to be travelling over "by himself" and after their arrival and he had checked into "his" hotel, he asked the crew members if they would like to "come to my room for a drink." Quite interested, they agreed and upon their arrival, David showed them the lovely view from his balcony and told them they could get a drink from the coke machine down the hall.

As if our sales staff didn't have enough work, Wardair purchased a second slightly-used 747 in December 1974 which took on the registration CF-FUN as our 727 had been sold. All its instrumentation was the same as on DJC and I could detect no difference from DJC when I flew it for the first time from Windsor down to Barbados.

As the decade wore on, Ian enrolled at York University in Toronto and used his family passes to fly from Vancouver to Toronto via either Honolulu or London, as Wardair even then was not allowed to fly passengers across Canada. Brian was attending Trinity Western College in

Langley as he was keen on learning to fly and David later studied at the University of Victoria.

Not to be outdone by our boys, Joy enrolled in the university's five-year French diploma course. As she had no opportunity to take French in High School, some of her earlier submissions to the cockpit written to me in Franglais were worth keeping! She graduated in 1985 and on our visit to France, many thought she was raised in Switzerland as she had a Swiss accent. Did I mention that I have no regrets over failing my first year of Grade 12 French?

After noticing that I had a two-day layover in England, I took Brenda (then 16) with me to London. After we arrived and had a quick sleep, the two of us toured downtown, had dinner and took in a stage show that evening. The following day, I rented a car and we drove around the countryside, ending up at a country pub for dinner and we flew home the next day. Jennifer at the age of 12 showed no interest in anywhere but Hawaii.

On February 10th 1975, I was called upon to carry out a three-engine ferry (empty) flight from Honolulu to Vancouver. I quickly discovered that FUN burned just as much fuel as it would have burned on four engines due to the extra drag and lower altitude involved. Then on May 19th, I flew a "5th pod" (a spare engine carried below the wing) from Vancouver to Prestwick to position it as our European spare. We flew at a lower than usual altitude due to the drag involved and burnt many more extra tons of fuel. However our passengers were quite intrigued by the sight of three engines hanging from the left wing. As a bonus, they also had better sightseeing at the lower altitude.

In 1976 I had a humbling experience flying a Cessna 185. I was flying from Edmonton south to Penhold with a Mission Aviation pilot and he asked me to try the landing on our return. I think I "landed" three times before finally bouncing onto the Edmonton runway. I kept thinking, "Gee but that runway is getting awfully close!"

Our second family dog was a purebred Golden Lab. We didn't realize that Duchess would be such a "shedder" until our vacuum cleaner started

5th engine. One way to ferry a spare engine was by using the "piggy-back" method. The engine pod was attached to "hard points" located beneath the wing.

protesting! Hair showed up everywhere and we finally had a built-in vacuum system installed to help with the clean-up job. Whenever we had company, one of my jobs was to clean the hair from our large (30 feet x 18 feet) living room floor. For some time, it remained a problem.

I took Joy with me to Gatwick whenever I had a few days layover and we often rented a car and drove all over beautiful southern England. One day we visited the famous Axminster Factory where they turn English wool into beautiful carpets. After conferring with their salesman, we chose a multi-coloured carpet that measured 24 x 12 feet and had it delivered to Gatwick. Wardair then carried it to Canada and it did yeoman service in our living room for decades. The dog hair blended in very nicely and our shedding problem, while not solved, was greatly reduced. Forty years later, that carpet is still doing yeoman service in our niece's home and showing little sign of wear.

We ran into an engine problem in April during our flight from Honolulu and landed in Vancouver with one shut down due to a bleed air valve problem. Several days later, just two hours out of Vancouver, we again shut the same engine down and returned to Vancouver. Regretfully, our spare engine was in Honolulu and we finally arrived there at midnight while nursing the sick engine, changed it for our spare, then flew to Calgary as passengers with the cranky one tucked safely under the left wing. The very next day, our crew flew the sick engine over to Prestwick with a fresh load of passengers. While our aircraft registration happened to be CF-FUN, believe me, those four days were not FUN.

During the Air Traffic Control (ATC) strike of August 1977, we were once again not allowed to fly in Canadian-controlled airspace, making for several interesting flights and circuitous detours. On August 8th, after our Vancouver passengers and crew were bussed to Seattle, we flew across the US to Boston for fuel, then eastward over the Atlantic Ocean keeping south of Canadian airspace. Our normal flying time of eight hours turned into eleven and our "duty day" was nearly twenty.

Approaching northern Canada on our return two days later, we descended to 28,000 feet to keep below controlled airspace on our way to Anchorage, our intended fuel stop. Our plan was then to fly offshore down to Seattle and exchange passengers there. However nearing Whitehorse, ATC called us with the news that the strike had ended! We climbed immediately to 39,000 feet and to the delight of our passengers, we eked out a flight direct to Vancouver (while looking at a possible fuel stop in Prince George). But when we arrived, we found that our outbound passengers and crew were not happy at all, as they had to fight all their way back from Seattle through customs and immigration to Vancouver before boarding their flight to Europe.

Canadian and British ATC actions continued into October and we and our passengers had to make various adjustments to our travel plans, many times using US and Norwegian (Trondheim) airspace to avoid the Canadian and British. We also positioned crews around Europe on various smaller aircraft under Visual Flight Rules such as the little deHavilland Heron, experiencing long duty days, and I logged almost a hundred hours of rather interesting flying.

In 1978, Wardair began flying from Toronto and Montreal to Malaga, Spain. Vancouver crews often operated to London, back to Toronto, across to Malaga, then up to London on a British-built Dart Herald which stopped to refuel halfway, resulting in extremely tiring five-day pairings. We carried our spare engine from London back to Toronto under our left wing on August 19th, taking the same time (and burning more fuel) as our earlier flight eastbound from Vancouver to Prestwick!

Upon receiving a free parking sticker for the Victoria airport, I bought a green 1970 Volvo P1800 sports car for use in commuting to the airport. That fall I had a two-week holiday and Joy and I enjoyed driving it down to San Diego to visit my old Air Force padre friend. It was great that he had a swimming pool for after we arrived, the weather became quite hot. The Volvo lacked air conditioning and we hurried home, not even stopping to take in the Reno Air Races which were then in progress. It was simply too hot for Joy who is not a hot weather person.

While the Volvo was really a fun car to drive, we had one female and three male drivers in our house (Ian was working in Edmonton),

My Volvo P1800. As the little boy ages, another albeit lesser love sometimes occurs!

all of whom enjoyed driving it as much as Joy and I did. One day, we three boys were going to the same place at the same time and being the smallest of the three, I was relegated to the back bench of *my* two-seat sports car! Much to our boys' disappointment, I sold it and have seen it occasionally since then, running around Victoria. It was a reluctant sale as Joy looked so cute in it!

When the Vancouver ferry terminal began charging to park on the causeway, I relied more heavily on "extra" seats of the commuter aircraft to fly home to Victoria where Joy or one of the boys would pick me up. One such pickup stands clearly in my memory. It was raining and quite late when I got off the aircraft and into the terminal building carrying my briefcase and bag and looked around for my wife. I saw her crouching behind a large garbage can, wearing her hat on backwards, dark sun glasses and making strange *psssst* sounds.

When I got closer, I started to ask what was going on but she just whispered, "Don't ask, just get me out of here."

After we climbed into the Hyundai, she sighed happily, then explained, "Part way out to the airport, I noticed a weird little thing on the dash that looked like a lamp a genie might jump out of and it was all lit up. This is a brand new car and our other cars didn't have things like that and I wondered all the way to the airport what it meant. I even tried rubbing it! When I got to the airport, I needed to use the washroom and when I got there, I was still puzzling about the light and didn't pay attention to the sign on the door. I walked into the mens' washroom and surprised a man at the urinal, fortunately with his back to me. He turned to look just as I figured out what that funny little light on the dash meant but I was so pleased that I had figured it out, I just yelled: 'I'm out of oil!' "

Suddenly realizing what she had just done, she turned frantically and ran into the ladies washroom. At this point, she combed her hair over her forehead, put her hat on backwards, added the shades, and turned her coat inside out, hoping the man wouldn't recognize her. Hiding behind the garbage can, she had a faint hope that no one would even notice her. As you may have already guessed, life has never been dull since the day I met her.

I had taken a great interest in geography in university and much enjoyed our westbound flights over northern Canada as we sped along over Canada's Northeast Passage and enjoyed sharing my interest with our passengers. One day I was returning on the ferry to Victoria in civilian clothes and happened to sit behind some of our English passengers who were describing their flight. I overheard one saying that while the Wardair service had been truly exceptional, the Captain seemed to have had too much to say, whereupon *this* captain curtailed future commentaries!

In June 1978, Wardair bought the first of two brand new 747s (XRA and XRD). With the need for more staff, I was appointed as a company check pilot and was put to work training our additional crews. Along with our check flight engineers, I was trained in the operation of the various 747 flight simulators in Seattle, San Francisco, Dallas and Toronto, and later in Vancouver, to check on and certify the competency of our pilots. On some months, I only occupied the rock-hard jump seat in the aircraft cockpit or stood behind the pilots in the simulator. The check pilots were themselves given a simulator ride every six months to renew their instrument rating by either the "Ministry of Trouble" or a company check pilot and no one knew when another checker would climb aboard to ride along with us.

Twice each year, flight crews are required to demonstrate their flying ability. After two hours of "warm-up" in the simulator in which various electrical and hydraulic faults are given along with practice in engine failures, an exercise was given which might go something like this: *Take-off at maximum gross weight (820,000 pounds) with an engine failure prior to the decision speed, then another take-off with a failure (or fire) just after decision speed necessitating a fuel dump to maximum landing weight and a return to land in marginal weather with a missed approach and a second engine failure and a landing. Another take-off and accelerated climb to high altitude with a pressurization leak and return for a third instrument approach and landing – usually after other electrical or hydraulic faults and another engine failure.*

While it got to be routine, we all gave it our best.

Simulator "flying" was not all work, of course, and we found it great fun frightening the pilots with a live insect, slowly being magnified 100 times and projected on the windscreen as the crew made their rather exacting approach into Los Angeles. Some of our more adventurous pilots also tried "landing" on the flight deck of a cruising aircraft carrier – a hopeless task! Along with our fellow DC-10 check pilots, we worked on "what if" procedures such as bringing our crippled aircraft to a belly landing at (or near) the Vancouver airport after losing all hydraulic power. I think the Vancouver Search and Rescue people would have had an immense task to rescue 470-odd people from the mud flats west of Vancouver.

I also carried out conversion pilot training on the 747 and one night practiced with two crews around the Abbotsford area in cloud without seeing the ground from take-off to landing. I also flew with crews to

Europe and Hawaii, ensuring they followed standard operating procedures. Peter, our chief flight engineer, had developed a marvellous
method of ensuring that every item on each checklist had been completed
which simplified our training and brought our flight operation to a much
higher standard for it eliminated accident-prone written checklists.

Although the jump seat was very upright and very hard, it was an
enjoyable job and I certainly learned a lot about the aircraft as I rode
back and forth with various crews. And several times, the Ministry of
Transport checked me as I was checking other pilots in the Toronto or
Vancouver simulators.

In May 1979, Wardair took delivery of our fifth 747 and during some
months after that, most of my work was "just" simulator instruction. The
200 series models were equipped with Rolls Royce engines of 60,000
pounds of thrust each and were very reliable. However no engines can
withstand a bird strike. One of our crews had such an incident just after
take-off from Victoria with an empty 200 series 747 bound for Vancouver
when an errant seagull totally destroyed one of those big (and very expensive) engines.

Wardair always prided itself on being the "on time" airline and
sometimes went to unusual lengths to maintain its reputation. On one
occasion, it was noted that the next crew to operate from London would
be unable to arrive in time for sufficient rest before their flight. Crew
scheduling therefore flew the entire 18 crew members down to New York
where they boarded a supersonic BA Concorde flight bound for London
and they had sufficient rest to operate their scheduled flight. I regretted
missing that opportunity of supersonic flight and had to wait until my
last year of airline flying to realize that experience, be it ever so briefly.

Once as we were approaching the Honolulu airport, we were held
high by the control tower until we were too high for our approach and
they offered us clearance for another circuit of the field while we lost
altitude. However, as we were flying a -200 series 747 with closed
cowls, we asked for a straight-in approach and *side-slipped* towards
the runway. This is usually done by lighter aircraft to kill altitude while

limiting airspeed. Our passengers on the left side had a lovely view of the approaching runway while those on the right had a lovely view of the hilly ridge to the north of the airport. Following our landing, the tower commented they had never seen that performed before with such a large aircraft.

Sometimes our Hawaiian layovers extended beyond a single day and crews rented cars for a drive around the island. Frequently we stopped at one of the beaches along the north shore for an exciting swim among the rolling breakers. On one occasion, I went for a swim with several others while non-swimmers in our party organized a light supper. I became separated from the other swimmers and made several attempts at getting back to the beach, only to be washed out by the high seas. I am a tolerably good swimmer and was not frightened as I paddled back and forth seeking calmer water. I was finally able to reach the beach some distance away where a creek was running into the ocean calming the breakers.

After making my way back to the group and finding my clothes, I found that two cars had already left as supper was over, night had fallen, and the third car was packing up to leave, having assumed that I was with the others. I had been in the water for a couple of hours and while very cold and tired, I was quite relieved that there had been no sharks about as they are attracted to the lights along the beach.

In 1980, Wardair was asked to provide numerous flights from Asia to bring "boat people" (refugees) to Canada and several of us check pilots flew to various Asian airports in January to scout the facilities and make hotel arrangements for our crews. Wardair crews from Toronto subsequently carried many thousands of so-called boat people to Montreal for our Canadian government, for we were capable of carrying many people on each 747 flight.

I took a great deal of interest "beating" flight plans sent to us by our navigators, once saving 32 minutes from Honolulu to Calgary and another time saving 28 minutes (and a far smoother flight) westbound from Frankfurt. On this flight, we flew north to Stavanger, Norway and to Jan Mayen Island and then along 76 degrees north latitude rather than the flight plan over Benbecula in the Hebrides Islands. On that path, we would have been battling strong headwinds and turbulence. Of course we had the great advantage of having more up to date wind forecasts.

After graduating from Trinity Western, our son Brian became a co-pilot with Time Air Airlines operating out of Hay River. I was privileged to fly with him from Lethbridge to Calgary on May 11th, 1982 in their four-engine DeHavilland Dash 7. After the flight, he regaled me with stories of how, in windy places such as Lethbridge and Medicine Hat, they simply use a logging chain for their windsocks!

While we had frequently used Victoria as our flight-planned alternate airport for Vancouver, the 747 had never landed there as the runway was just 7,000 feet long and we weren't sure about the runway strength. One evening therefore, I climbed the control tower stairs and checked with the tower operators that our maximum landing and take-off weights were within their runway and taxiway limits which indeed they were and we were told that our Victoria landings would be most welcome.

To the chagrin of our Vice President of Flight Operations who wanted to be the first, on September 29th, 1981, I planted the wheels of DJC on the Victoria runway and used it for pilot training in both "touch and go's" and full stop landings. My first 747 passenger flight through Victoria occurred more than a year later, on November 7th, 1982 when I piloted XRA from Edmonton to Victoria, then on to Honolulu with 456 happy passengers. After this, we flew many charters through Victoria to Honolulu and then back to the Prairies, picking up or dropping half our loads in each place.

At that time, Victoria had only a small passenger terminal which was barely suitable to handle 100 passengers at a time. It had an open air baggage rack out on the ramp from which the passengers retrieved their checked baggage. For loading and unloading half our 456-passenger load, a two-storey passenger stairway had to be brought over from Vancouver whenever we were expected, and the fuel company had to be reminded to fill their trucks! But the crews very much enjoyed overlooking the "wee terminal" from our third-storey windows as we taxied up to it.

Above: *Approaching Victoria. Our early morning view of Runway 26 from the cockpit.*

Below: *One of our many 747 flights approaches the Victoria Airport at dawn carrying half our passenger load from the Prairies. Wheels and flaps are down and Mt. Baker is in the background. Departure for Honolulu occurred as soon as the other half had boarded.*

Once the company discovered how easy it was to operate from 7,000-foot runways, they scheduled us into many others – mostly in the UK. These included Birmingham, Leeds-Bradford, Cardiff in Wales, and Newcastle-on-Tyne and we always drew admiring crowds who had never seen such large aircraft at their airports before. When flying longer distances, because of our heavier fuel loads, we could only depart from airports with longer runways. For example, our sales staff had us drop half our passengers in Birmingham and the other half in Gatwick before picking up a full load there for Western Canada.

While I had never smoked, smoking had always been allowed in our aircraft cockpits, as well as in our simulators and I developed polyps on my vocal cords. However I was grateful that, while I was put to sleep and had the polyps removed several times, I was still able to carry on flying, just becoming more hoarse and "growly" with age. Smoke was a nuisance, not just for us non-smokers, but also for our aircraft's instrumentation. When all flights became non-smoking, our maintenance people were much happier, as valves and instruments required much less servicing.

While Wardair was still not allowed to carry passengers across Canada, there was nothing to stop us from carrying freight. Our sales people were not idle and we carried many tons of freight across Canada and, in addition to our full passenger loads, frequently flew with tons of freight "down below" internationally as well. Several times I brought 20-ton loads of freight from Honolulu to Vancouver. In May 1983, I carried 25 tons from Calgary to Toronto, and after working in the simulator and doing some flying training, I returned to Vancouver with 12 tons of freight, carried out more simulator training there, then drove to the ferry and finally arrived back in Victoria.

Wardair operated "pilgrim flights" during the Hadj to and from such diverse places as Casablanca and India. I was in Cairo both in September 1982 and again in October 1983 and flew a half dozen flights to Jedda (near Mecca). In flight, I witnessed attempts by individuals to light fires in the aisle to cook their mid-day meals! And the sound they gave when deplaning in Jedda was indeed quite memorable.

All was not without the "usual" 747 problems and we experienced several engine compressor stalls on our flight to Honolulu on January 5th 1984, finally shutting the offending engine down. Passengers were not aware of our inoperative engine and we started it up and had it running again for our landing. After its settings were adjusted and tested, it ran smoothly once more for the return trip.

At one of our Wardair get-togethers, Joy and I won the draw for a return ticket to Hong Kong on Cathay Pacific Airlines. After some planning for our holiday, we arrived in Hong Kong and in three days enjoyed many of its tourist attractions.

We then took a Thai Airlines flight to Bangkok, visited the famous floating market and took a long-tailed boat for some sightseeing. Three days later, we boarded a high-speed Canadian-built train northbound to a small village south of Chiang Mai for a visit with our seven-year-old Christian Children's Fund "daughter." James Bond in Thai was the feature film that day and the hot dinner was excellent but Joy's description of her visit to the lavatory (which was simply a hole in the floor) while wearing a one-piece jumpsuit was quite hilarious. The meeting with our little adoptee and her family was just as seen in the movie *The King and I*, and a Third World experience which we'll always cherish. Returning to Vancouver, we were seated in Cathay's smoking section and the non-smokers, such as Joy who had a heavy cold, suffered greatly.

I have been asked if I ever hit an "air pocket". While our DC-6 flights south of Honolulu had often suffered heavy turbulence, I really had no idea what an air pocket was until, during our flight to Honolulu on January 17th in turbulence, I experienced what might be termed an "elevator drop" of some 700 feet as our altimeters, and my logbook, recorded. While it was a relatively smooth fall during a particularly rough patch, it was fortunate that our passengers and crew had been strapped in while this was occurring. We only broke a few pieces of our Royal Doulton china.

We carried hundreds of tons of freight that summer and also operated to and from many of the smaller English airports. For example, on July 12th I left Toronto at 7:30 pm for Birmingham where half our passengers deplaned, then hopped over to Cardiff, Wales where the other half got off. Our crew then climbed into the little Brazilian-built Embraer Bandeirante aircraft parked beside us which took us to Prestwick for a sleep so we would be prepared for the next day's flight to Calgary where half our passengers deplaned and we then carried on to Vancouver, arriving there at 1:30 pm on July 14th. I couldn't imagine how our efficient staff scrambled to arrange all those flights.

As a check pilot on September 22nd, I sat on FUN's hard jump seat behind the pilots to Calgary and on to Prestwick where I caught a BA Trident aircraft to London followed by a 737 flight to Frankfurt. I slept, then rode DJC's hard seat behind another crew back to Calgary and on to Vancouver. One could really call that type of flying "hard" work.

January 1985 saw us in the holding pattern over the Vancouver airport several times for persistent winter fog followed by auto-pilot controlled "Category 2" landings as the slowly-lifting fog permitted. As fog meant expensive delays as well as additional fuel (3,000 gallons an hour!), we tried our best to maintain our schedule.

During the summer, we operated to and from Abbotsford while the main Vancouver runway was being resurfaced. Our passengers transferred to and from a string of busses directly to and from the aircraft while their baggage was being transferred and our schedule was adjusted to account for the extra time involved.

In August after leaving Frankfurt, we were forced to return in order to deplane an unruly passenger – my first and, I think, my only one! However, as we were only bound for Toronto with a partial load, we didn't need to dump fuel and simply landed near our maximum landing weight, refuelled and, one costly passenger and his baggage lighter, departed again.

On March 10th 1986, I was busy in the Vancouver simulator when Joy called to say that my mother had suddenly passed away that morning at her recent home in Victoria. I very gladly handed my job to another check pilot who had been flying the simulator that day and scrambled for home.

On September 19th, we were en route from Manchester to Toronto when we were advised that we had a medical emergency onboard and so diverted into Halifax, our closest airport, and our passenger was rushed to hospital. I never heard about his outcome. And, unlike our DC-6 days where lighting strikes had been regular occurrences, now every lightning strike was duly recorded. On October 26th, 1986 I logged a particularly blinding flash as we were leaving Frankfurt for Vancouver and believed we had been struck. However after a careful check in Vancouver, no damage was found.

Another requirement was to log an autopilot landing on every aircraft at least once every month, thus ensuring that the aircraft was prepared to land automatically when the ceiling was as low as 100 feet and/or the visibility was as low as 1,200 feet. In March of 1987, I passed the quarter century mark with Wardair and was awarded my diamond lapel pin which I still treasure.

As she had done in Edmonton, Joy became the "mother confessor" to the many children in our neighbourhood. Many teens have her to thank for advice and instruction in their life skills. When fathers were working and mothers were out shopping or with their crowd, the teens found the warm cinnamon buns very appealing and anyone who needed it, was mothered.

In the summer of 1987, to get my monthly flying hours in a short period and leaving more time at home, I bid on the rather brutal run that went from Vancouver to Frankfurt followed by a 4-hour wait for our positioning flight on Lufthansa Airlines to Paris Orly after a stop in Dusseldorf. Then came a rather lengthy bus ride to our hotel near Paris Le Bourget for our 9 o'clock departure next morning to either Quebec City or Montreal, and then on to Toronto. The following evening saw us off to Manchester followed by a positioning flight to London and we finally arrived back in Vancouver on the fifth day!

Our Paris Le Bourget operation was interesting, for we were directed to our parking place between the hangars which was a very tight fit for our 747. Of course we had very experienced ground personnel to guide us in as we could not see our wing tips. Many years later, I parked our pickup truck in very tight quarters under our condo and the ladies there told everyone that I had no problem "but of course he was used to parking a 747."

On our flight on October 15th from Toronto, we carried a full load of passengers to Prestwick, dropped half there and then left for Gatwick. As we climbed, Air Traffic Control advised us that the Gatwick Airport had been closed as a hurricane was then passing eastward along the English Channel. We diverted into Manchester where the winds were already blowing 40 knots and gusting much higher while the altimeter setting, as the Manchester tower kept informing us, was a "LOW, LOW 28.62 inches". They wanted to be absolutely certain that we were fully prepared. It was an interesting landing to say the least but as we drew up to the terminal, we were informed that busses were already on their way. What an efficient ground staff.

In like manner, one of our flights experienced an engine problem two hours out of Honolulu, forcing it to return. Arriving back at the ramp, 11 buses were waiting to take the 450 passengers and crew to hotel rooms which had been arranged by our super staff.

I think the highlight of my flying career occurred on February 19th, 1988 on a flight to Honolulu. After gaining experience with Time Air, our son Brian had been flying Wardair's Airbus 300 for some time before "graduating" onto the 747. On this flight, Brian was my co-pilot and did a beautiful landing in Honolulu. As we coasted to taxi speed and turned off the runway, I proudly told our passengers that my son had done that landing. Shortly thereafter, a stewardess (sorry, cabin attendant) burst into the cockpit to ask that I announce that my son Brian was a fully certified 747 pilot and not just some little 6-year-old sitting on his daddy's knee!

We were warmly welcomed by our Honolulu staff who presented us

Above: *An auspicious first father-son 747 team en route to Honolulu.*

Below: *A lei greeting following arrival in Honolulu after our epic flight.*

with leis. As far as we know, we were the very first father-son team to fly Boeing's 747 together in passenger service. It was certainly an airline first. We flew together the rest of the week, sharing "nuisances" such as a flat tire and a hydraulic leak. And the following month, we spent another enjoyable week together, flying back and forth to Honolulu.

Few people have experienced the satisfaction of breaking free from cloud at minimum altitude with the runway just ahead. Still fewer have experienced the thrill of lifting the nose of their aircraft into a flying position for take-off and "feeling the air" as it gently accepts its 410-ton burden. And fewer still have enjoyed the satisfaction of doing so while seated beside their pilot son!

On October 7th, I flew to Manchester with Joy as my passenger for a four-day "working holiday", then returned to Vancouver where I demonstrated a fully automatic landing (and braking). Then on October 20th, I flew to Frankfurt for a six-day working holiday, again with Joy as a passenger, and on October 31st, I flew to Honolulu, once again with Joy as a passenger, for another four-day holiday. It was certainly a most enjoyable month of "working holidays".

But then a real emergency occurred on November 4th as we were returning with a full load of passengers and Joy seated in the jump seat behind me. It had been an unseasonably hot day and it was a long distance taxiing all the way from the Honolulu terminal out to the reef runway. We had almost reached our waiting spot for take-off beside this runway when a bright red light on our engineer's panel indicated a *FIRE* in our aft cargo compartment!

We quickly notified the tower and one after the other discharged the two big fire extinguisher bottles into the cargo hold. The tower advised us that the fire crew was on the way and it arrived, fully clothed in their asbestos suits, in an amazingly scant 45 seconds! To this day, I remain in awe of their speed.

While our standard operating procedures called for an immediate aircraft evacuation, I had visions of our untrained passengers sliding down our eleven steep evacuation slides. So when the fire chief called up on the inter-phone, I requested that they first feel the aft compartment door, then take a peek inside. When he called back to say that indeed there was no fire, our entire crew breathed a *tremendous* sigh of relief. We taxied back to the ramp, unloaded our passengers and baggage, recharged both extinguisher bottles, replaced our defective fire warning sensor and had an uneventful flight home.

Max was waiting for us with the Boeing engineers and, following their consultation, immediately decided to install a backup fire detection loop as was installed in our 200 series aircraft. I believe we avoided many injuries and even saved lives that day, but it was certainly a very fortunate call with so many lives hanging on that decision.

Undaunted, Joy flew with me to Honolulu on the 24th, again for another four days on the beach. And Brian flew with me to Honolulu several times that winter, including several flights carrying VIPs. We also flew together several times to Europe during the summer of 1989 and then to Honolulu that winter. It was indeed, a most enjoyable year.

Following one of my last 747 flights, I was greeted by our oldest grandson who had just turned five. He had driven out to the airport with Joy only after insisting that he be allowed to wear his flying suit!

My final flight on the 747, also with Wardair, was quite anticlimactic, for I flew from Honolulu to Calgary on April 15th, 1990 and returned to Vancouver the following morning as a CPA passenger and quietly caught the ferry home, having flown 7,214 hours in my favourite aircraft, Boeing's Queen of the Skies, the 747.

As a PS, I had also "flown" 530 hours in the various completely realistic, full-motion 747 flight simulators.

CANADIAN AIRLINES

Wardair was sold to the PWA Corporation back in 1989 which was then in the process of amalgamating six Canadian airlines to compete with the Air Canada giant. The amalgamated airline was called Canadian Airlines and I was assigned to fly Wardair's Airbus A310, of which Wardair had 12 at the time, with more on order. While I had been a passenger in one of our Airbuses in May 1989 when I flew to Toronto for our annual 747 ground school refresher and again the following February for our semi-annual simulator training, I had not visited the cockpit.

My A310 ground school course took place in Toronto in May 1990 accompanied by our son Brian. We were very pleased to discover that the aircraft was a non-smoking aircraft and we truly enjoyed its clean air. But we missed yet another of our cockpit crew as our Flight Engineer had been dispensed with, leaving just the two pilots. I had some trouble converting to its "glass cockpit," stupidly not realizing what "profile climb" and "profile descent" meant and Brian thankfully came to my rescue. Then in June came 36 hours of totally realistic simulator flying with daylight and a full-colour visual presentation, ending with the inevitable certification ride by a Ministry of Transport Inspector.

The A310 was equipped with a GPS (Global Positioning System) of navigation which was far more accurate than the INS system we had in our 747s and became so refined that in later years it enabled aircrews to

Father and son flying a Canadian Airlines Airbus A310. Another airline but the same team!

"build" their own approaches to any airport completely independent of expensive ground-based systems.

July 5th, 1990 marked my first A310 flight in a real aircraft. I was paired with a first officer who, like myself, had never before seen the "front office" of the real aircraft which we noted had been painted in the new Canadian Airlines colours. We two totally "green" pilots climbed into the cockpit, buckled ourselves in and started the aircraft engines, then carried 180 totally unsuspecting passengers from Vancouver to Toronto. We did, however, carry a check pilot along in the jump seat behind us "in case we got into any trouble."

On our return to Calgary which was then basking in sunny "Stampede Weather," all went well until we were on our final approach and the runway in use was changed by the control tower due to a wind shift. I simply cancelled all the aircraft's whiz-bang computer approach systems and reverted to a simple manual landing and the aircraft seemed to perform just as the ground school and simulator had advertised.

As our entire A310 fleet was based in Toronto, the Vancouver crews mostly flew the domestic route across Canada. I was able to pair up with son Brian that fall on a series of flights which began in Calgary and proceeded to Toronto, Halifax, back to Toronto, Montreal, Toronto and ended in Vancouver.

Occasionally however, we flew to the Caribbean when needed and in March 1991, we were flying down to Barbados from Toronto when we crossed paths with another of our A310s which, at the time, was on its way back to Toronto. It was indeed a very pretty sight.

One truly awesome experience occurred during our night flight from Calgary to Toronto when the weather briefing had included the sentence: "A line of heavy thunderstorm activity can be expected between Winnipeg and London" (Ontario). As we barrelled along in a friendly jet stream approaching Winnipeg at 37,000 feet, Air Traffic Control advised us that all eastbound traffic had thus far been requesting a re-routing well to the south of this heavy thunderstorm activity.

We were riding the jet-stream at the time in smooth air, being pushed along by 150 mph winds. But in the blackness ahead of us, despite the flickering lights of lightning, we noticed in the moonlight that our present path would lead us between two long columns of cloud whose tops were well above our altitude and I decided that we should "go for it!" And so, tying everything and everyone down in the back, we entered that "long black tunnel" which was perhaps two or three miles wide.

With Air Traffic's permission to deviate as required, we sped along this long corridor in perfectly smooth air while almost constant lightning played between the clouds on both sides of the aircraft – a truly awesome sight for our passengers when the cabin attendants dimmed the lights. In fact, I don't recall seeing any stars or moon above us, probably due to the nearly constant lightning. We notified Air Traffic Control of our experience and other aircraft decided to follow our path through those "footless halls of air." That we arrived in Toronto many minutes ahead of schedule was just icing on the cake.

One of my flights happened to be a night positioning flight from Calgary to Vancouver. With our empty aircraft, our climb was rapidly normal at several thousand feet per minute until, passing through 38,000 feet, our 120-mph head wind suddenly ceased, our airspeed just as suddenly dropped, and we literally "fell out of the sky" in a classic low speed stall. Re-entering the jet-stream as we fell out of the sky, our airspeed increased very rapidly indeed and we briefly exceeded the speed of sound (as registered on our mach meters) before regaining normal flight. Thankfully, our flight attendants were all seated at the time with seat belts fastened. The aircraft was thoroughly checked over upon our arrival in Vancouver and just as thankfully, no damage or undue stresses were found. However I can quite truthfully boast that I have indeed "gone supersonic."

Later that fall, I experienced one of the few times I have had an extensive delay on the Airbus due to a mechanical problem. One engine showed vibration on start-up in Toronto and a close inspection determined that an engine change was required. Thankfully we were at our main base and a spare was available, although our flight to Calgary was delayed for several hours.

Government regulations at the time required that I retire from flying upon reaching the ripe old age of 60. My last flight with Canadian Airlines was sadly a copy of my last flight with Wardair – quite anticlimactic, for I returned from Toronto to Vancouver on October 20th, 1991 as a humble passenger, seated quietly on one of our rear passenger seats.

It was quite apparent to us all that an amalgamated airline was certainly a long shot, for it took on the burden of amalgamating *six* airlines, all with different aircraft and spares, different checklists and procedures, different counter staff, different uniforms, and differing cockpit philosophies. While it could quickly change outward appearances, it could not channel the differences built up over the years, and purchase a whole new fleet of aircraft in a brief period of time with very little cash.

In any event, I was only with Canadian Airlines for little more than a year until, with twenty-nine years and eleven months of service with Canadian Pacific/Wardair/Canadian, I was officially retired. My mandatory retirement occurred nearly a decade before "9/11" and all the security measures which followed which have taken so much enjoyment out of flying, for both passengers and crew. I logged just 676 hours in my single year of flying the A310.

Five from our fleet of 12 Airbus 310s which I had flown were sold to Canada's military. Passing Vancouver airport one day, our son Brian happened to witness the action as one of these was driven into a hangar at full power after one of the mechanics bypassed an "on the ground" circuit on an engine check. The aircraft, "thinking" it was airborne at far too low an airspeed, went to full power (the throttles didn't move!) jumped its chocks and shot forward into the hangar.

Rather than trashing the aircraft as recommended by Airbus Industries, the military patched it up and flew it unpressurized to Toulouse France where Airbus converted it into a cargo-carrying A310 now known as the CC-150 Polaris. A total of four now carry that designation, two of which are also used as aerial tankers for our CF18s. The fifth of our 310's inside was refinished and became the VIP aircraft which has been used to carry Canada's Prime Ministers all over the world.

MISSION AVIATION

W anting to still be of some use at the "tender" age of 60 and still with a valid licence, I applied as a volunteer with MAFC (Mission Aviation Flying of Canada) as a relief pilot. On February 20th, 1992, I was checked out on a light twin turboprop Beechcraft King Air 100 in London, Ontario, and in June was sent to Angola to relieve one of the MAFC pilots who was going out on furlough.

I packed a good supply of hypodermic needles and other medical supplies – for we had been told that Angola was very short of them – and then had a complicated time taking them through Vancouver airport security! Joy also gave me a number of spices to pack as we heard that they were impossible to obtain.

Mine was a very long trip, for I flew from Vancouver to London, England on a Canadian Airlines aircraft and four hours later, flew to Brussels with Sabena Airlines and then transferred to one of their Africa-bound 747s. After its doors were closed, I slowly came to the realization that I was the sole white person on board! And the smell from the rancid hairdos was quite oppressive (they used butter as a hair conditioner).

We flew a circuitous route outside the western side of Africa to Kinshasa, Congo and finally into Luanda, the seaside capital of Angola. We were warned that taking any photographs in Angola was strictly forbidden. My checked baggage took three additional weeks to arrive – for some reason it was sent via Karachi, Pakistan.

The other MAF pilot and I were billeted with two nurses in Luanda on the northwestern coast of Angola. Iris and Becky kept a small house in which electricity was very intermittent and used our aviation jet fuel for their stove and fridge. Water was trucked in and fed into a huge tank on stilts in the back yard, heated daily by the sun. Early morning risers just had cool showers!

The nurses also had a shipping container, half of which held basic medical supplies and the prescription drugs used by their rudimentary first aid outpost. This was visited from time to time by a Canadian doctor who came from the hospital at Kalekembe either by MAF flights when available, or by a torturous drive in a Volvo which had 1/4-inch armour plating on its underside for protection against land mines. Twenty million of these mines were planted throughout Angola, preventing agricultural activities for many decades to come. The other half of the container provided living quarters for MAF's radio technician and his family.

It was quite an experience flying the pressurized King Air during the brief lull in the ongoing civil war between UNITA (backed by the USA) and the MPLA (supported by Russia and Cuba). We became used to calling on the common frequency 126.7 mcs following take-off and climbing rapidly to our 25,000-foot cruising altitude to avoid small arms fire. We radioed again on reaching cruising altitude, kept a vigilant watch en route, called again when starting our descent and finally after landing.

We used a very basic GPS receiver to find our many destinations such as Luena, Huambo, Benguela, Malange, Lubango, Menongue, Kuito and Uige. We carried supplies and personnel for the United Nations on Mondays, Wednesdays and Fridays and relief supplies and personnel on Tuesdays, Thursdays and Saturdays. MAF was also permitted to use all unoccupied seats on every UN flight.

On one of our flights to Uige, northeast of Luanda, we had unloaded our UN supplies and were landing back at Luanda when three MIGS performed a victory roll over the airfield and landed behind us. We later heard that they had blown up our UN supplies with machine gun fire and killed several of their workers!

MAF's Beechcraft at Uige airport in Angola. A country at war with itself is never a pretty picture. A country ravaged by war for decades will never fully recover.

We flew south as far as Rundu across the border in northern Namibia where we enjoyed a "real store," and could purchase "real food" and badly-needed equipment parts. Trying to spot wild game en route was a hopeless task at our cruising altitude. Even on a subsequent trip from Rundu as a passenger in one of our Cessna Caravans, we could spot nothing even though we were flying at a low altitude on an unusually quiet day. We also attended a worship service at an outdoor amphitheater outside of Luanda with 4,000 others. The language spoken was primarily Portuguese which most people understood.

I arrived home with both my bags and memories and with the firm conviction that everyone should visit the third world, hopefully before leaving school, for it would certainly make us all appreciate what we have here in Canada.

RETIREMENT?

S hortly after returning from Angola, I spied a newspaper article say- ing that the Canadian government was searching for qualified DC-3 pilots to operate their coastal patrol flights. Shortly after that, I saw their Gooney Bird flying by overhead and broached the subject to Joy who burst out with, "Surely you're not suggesting gallivanting about the skies again in that sixty-year-old bucket of bolts!"

And so squashed, I never applied.

During my flying career, I had been blessed with good health and good eyesight, as attested by my semi-annual medicals and the fact that I had never booked off a single flight in 40 years due to health reasons. I seem to have saved my problems with hearing loss, hoarse voice, smashed hip and prostate cancer until many years after I retired!

In the fall of 1992, Joy organized a big surprise retirement party for me in our home, to which many Wardair friends were invited and kind words were said. While Max and Marjorie Ward declined to come due to business pressures, they said they would drop by sometime later. True to their word, Max phoned us one day and invited us to have dinner with them. At the appointed time, they flew into the Victoria Airport in their Canadian-built Challenger jet and took us to dinner at the Stone House Restaurant in Sidney. They were flying between Edmonton and Calgary and had made a "small detour" to Victoria to visit us! After dinner, Max delighted in showing us his "toy jet" before they took off.

We had heard that the thing to do after one's retirement is to take a trip. For our retirement trip, we bought a small fifth wheel and truck. After a few trial runs, we set off in 1997 for a trip across Canada and the USA. We drove east across Canada, seeing friends and stopping at various camping grounds before spending some time in the Maritimes. We enjoyed the exotic fall colours in the Annapolis Valley and such places as Baddeck, NS where we visited the Alexander Graham Bell Museum. We then flew to Newfoundland where we visited Cape Spear – the easternmost point of land in North America, 5070 kilometres by air from Victoria.

Driving down the East Coast as winter approached, we visited the site of the Wright Brothers' first flight at Kitty Hawk, North Carolina and drove south as far as Tallahassee, Florida before turning west, crossing the southern States and visiting New Orleans and then wintering in Harlingen, Texas. There we saw many interesting animals such as armadillos and javelinas, and birds such as green jays.

On the way home, we stayed at Big Bend National Park on the Rio Grande for a few days before viewing the Grand Canyon from a rather draughty Cessna 172 that took us up on a sightseeing tour. After eight months "on the road," we agreed that it had been the trip of a lifetime.

A few years later, 18 of us were invited to the Ward's fishing camp at Redrock Lake off the Coppermine River west of Contwoyto Lake. Max himself flew us up to "his lake" in his DeHavilland Twin Otter floatplane from Yellowknife. For several days in August, we spent a most enjoyable time at his cabin in fine weather, ending up with a delectable fish BBQ on the beach.

In 2012, one of Wardair's original pilots living in Edmonton organized a 50th anniversary celebration of Wardair's startup in that city. Many of our "old-timers" attended this Wardair family party and all of us, including Max and Marjorie Ward, enjoyed the many tales of Wardair that were recounted. It was a great time of happy reminisces and laughter.

While in Edmonton, I visited the Aviation Museum at Edmonton's Municipal Airport and much enjoyed the memories as I sat in the *very*

CPA's 55-year-old DC-6 simulator cockpit. Memories of a bygone era!

same DC-6 simulator on which I had worked diligently with the CPA pilots fifty years before in Vancouver. Like me, those pilots have long ago been retired and have received their "Crystal Goose," one of which sits today on our mantlepiece.

A very happy flying moment occurred when Joy and I flew to London Heathrow as passengers on our first Boeing 777 flight. Following our arrival at the ramp, son Brian invited us into "his cockpit" and proudly showed us around. He had just completed the landing which was, of course, a perfectly smooth "Wardair" landing.

In 2014 while at the Palm Springs Air Museum, I sat once more in the cockpit of a C-119 "Flying Boxcar" which seemed to be such a small and very basic aircraft. Then the following year, I sat in the cockpit of a Boeing 314 "Clipper" flying boat at Foynes, Ireland which had been flying across the Atlantic at the beginning of WW2 and is one of the few Boeing passenger aircraft that between Brian and myself, we have not flown. Together we have flown eight Boeing jets: the 707, 727, 737, 747, 757/767, 777 and the 787.

My life in flight has unfolded from canvas-covered Piper Cub with a 65-hp engine carrying two at 80 mph… through the DC-3 weighing 29,000 pounds with a crew of five seating 26 passengers at 150 mph… to the 747 weighing 820,000 pounds with a crew of perhaps 21 carrying 456 passengers at 560 mph. Happy memories!

What more could a person want from life beyond a happy marriage, a wonderful family and a satisfying career?

And how does an ex-pilot "feel" the wind after retirement? He goes sailing over the ocean naturally! After graduating from a sailing school, owned and run by Captain James Cook (if you please), our first boat was an Omega trimaran – not only excitingly fast but also uncomfortably wet! Joy did one racing gybe that parted my hair as the boom shot over. She laid down that our next boat had to have both a stove and a toilet, so we bought a Sunstar 28 – not as fast or as thrilling but we could still "enjoy" feeling the wind and it had a outdoor solar shower, a stove, and a "head"! We have seen elephant seals and participated in scuba diving (in which Joy excelled), watched the fish, seals and swimming scallops. However Joy didn't enjoy the foredeck work on the sailboat – deploying foresails and lifting the anchor, so our third purchase was a North Sea 34

Joy diving from our North Sea 34 in Desolation Sound. Brandy was already in the water.

which was a motor sailer with a propane fridge, a furnace, a furling jib and an anchor winch.

The natural question arises when one is boating out on the Pacific Ocean: Didn't we ever go fishing? Having tried it once with disastrous results, I was reluctant to try again, but try I did – both with friends and alone. While I enjoy eating fish, I discovered that fishing and I just don't get along together. I remain content to buy a freshly cleaned fish from the professionals at the wharf.

For several years we sailed our North Sea 34 to Desolation Sound where, in the warm ocean waters we much enjoyed swimming (and Joy can still swim a mile). We had an English cocker spaniel at the time and after Joy dove off the boat and swam some distance, Brandy would jump in and, with legs going like little pistons, would pass her, then glance behind seemingly saying, "What's keeping you?"

We frequently traversed the rapids beyond Desolation, reaching as far as Port McNeill on the north coast of Vancouver Island. One of our

*Gartshore family photo. Front row, from left – Jennifer, Joy, David. Back row –
Brenda, Bob, Ian, Brian.*

memorable sails was "wing on wing" in 20 knot winds eastbound along
Queen Charlotte Strait in thick fog using our radar to avoid the fishing boats with their lines all deployed. Navigation was quite basic but
we enjoyed the luxury of anchoring for the night in quiet coves, with a
comfortable bed always ready.

For many years, a group of our Wardair boater friends attended a
"boat-in" when as many as 7 boats were rafted together in some quiet
bay as we enjoyed each other's company, and of course there were many
tall flying tales passed around.

While waterborne craft were fun and even exciting at times, I must
confess that I miss the three-dimensional freedom of true flight. From our
condo's patio overlooking the ocean, I watch the eagles and seagulls as
they circle lazily about to take advantage of the updrafts, herons as they
plod across our bay in *ground effect*, crows as they extend their legs and

tilt their wings for a *branch landing,* geese as they take full advantage of the added lift provided kindly by their leaders, ducks as they splash into the water after a full stall, and swallows as they dart about keeping perfectly tight formation. I now know what all those feel like!

One afternoon while experiencing very strong gusty winds, we watched as hundreds of seagulls performed a series of climbing, turning and then diving manoeuvres as they streamed down through the pack of their fellow gulls, leaving us quite awestruck. They were obviously having a great deal of fun just playing in the strong gusty wind, but how they avoided collisions was quite beyond us.

I have been asked why I don't take up flying model aircraft. There is an active club not far away, and while I enjoy their great annual show, I believe there is nothing that will take the place of air supporting the human being. Does the retired hockey player really enjoy playing computer hockey?

I freely acknowledge that throughout my life, it has been the Lord God who has guided my words and actions every time I have given Him control, for He is a far better pilot than I will ever be. He is certainly *not* my co-pilot but my constant companion! He has also given me many gifts, the best one being Joy, and He allowed us to celebrate our Diamond Jubilee together, surrounded by loving family.

As the years passed, my Joy developed a beautiful singing voice. For our 62nd anniversary on Sunday, May 29th, 2016, I asked her to sing *"Ride the Morning Wind"* for me in church that morning. For some reason I insisted, even though she protested, saying that she had developed a "frog in her throat." But she finally relented and I had it recorded, frog and all.

Four days later, as I was proof-reading this manuscript, my Joy, my wonderful partner, died suddenly and left me....

HIGH FLIGHT

by John Gillespie Magee, Jr

Oh! I have slipped the surly bonds of earth,
And danced the skies on laughter-silvered wings;
Sunward I've climbed, and joined the tumbling mirth
Of sun-split clouds, — and done a hundred things
You have not dreamed of — wheeled and soared and swung
High in the sunlit silence. Hov'ring there
I've chased the shouting wind along, and flung
My eager craft through footless halls of air....

Up, up the long, delirious, burning blue
I've topped the wind-swept heights with easy grace
Where never lark or even eagle flew —
And, while with silent lifting mind I've trod
The high untrespassed sanctity of space,
Put out my hand, and touched the face of God.

EPILOGUE

As the sun sank toward the horizon and shadows lengthened, a solitary speck could be seen off in the distance long before any sound could be heard. As the speck grew larger, interested observers at the aerodrome noted that this speck was actually two aircraft flying together in close formation.

In the calm evening air, the pair arrowed swiftly toward the airfield and, as they approached, they slowed as flaps were lowered. In the setting sun, wheels were extended. As the turn onto final approach was made, full flap slowed the pair further until, over the end of the runway, still stitched together, they seemed to be barely moving.

Touchdowns were simultaneous and feather-light and, as speed brakes were extended, the two aircraft continued to roll slower and slower until a turnoff could be made and flaps were retracted. The two taxied in tandem to the apron where a small knot of people waited patiently, then wheeled into parking position as onlookers turned their backs against the hot jet exhaust. Brakes were set and engine noise died away as fuel was cut off.

As quiet descended and twilight deepened, those around the aircraft pointed to the chipped paint, dented wings and cowls, a cracked windscreen and a missing fairing with the comment that the pair must have been through a great deal of weather together.

Hangar doors were opened and tugs pushed both machines tail first inside as observers trailed behind. As the aircraft faced the closing doors in the gathering darkness, one onlooker turned to his friend with the remark, "What memories those two must have had!"

Although these have been my memories, the flight has been *ours*.

Made in the USA
San Bernardino, CA
29 November 2017